HOW TO SPEAK WITH THE DEAD

HOW TO SPEAK
WITH THE DEAD
: : A PRACTICAL HANDBOOK : :

By Sciens

AUTHOR OF RECOGNISED SCIENTIFIC
TEXT-BOOKS

Cur℩ous
PUBLICATIONS
New York

Published by Curious Publications
101 W. 23rd St. #318
New York, NY 10011
curiouspublications.com

Originally published in 1918, by E. P. Dutton & Co.

Cover art by Lela Hartzman.

ISBN-13: 978-1-7353201-0-6

Printed and bound in the United States of America.

A Note on the Text

This edition reprints the 1918 publication of *How to Speak with the Dead: A Practical Handbook*, written anonymously by "Sciens."

Before you begin your training, you'll find a review of the book from a 1919 issue of *Life Magazine*. The reviewer claims that Sciens has "so simplified the process that it is within easy reach of all." That said, Curious Publications guarantees no results.

A review from *Life Magazine*,
October 9, 1919.

A GUIDE TO
GHOST SEEING

OR

EVERY MAN HIS OWN
MEDIUM

By Agnes Repplier

A LONG-FELT want has been supplied by the publication of a "Practical Handbook" (E. P. Dutton & Co.), to be used in communicating with spirits. Not that we lave lacked literature on this inspiring theme. LIFE itself has called attention to the extent and variety of our information. But the anonymous author of "How to Speak with the Dead" has so simplified the process that it is within easy reach of all. A pad and a pencil for automatic writing, a tumbler and a key, in case the ghostly visitant prefers to call in the dark. With this inexpensive equipment any man or woman may hold an "expectancy sitting" in the privacy of home—the hours between midnight and two A. M. being best adapted to this form of social intercourse.

Larger gatherings are not, however, discountenanced. On the contrary, an "expectancy circle" which comes together regularly and punctually, which provides a table for rapping, and seeks the cordial "cooperation" of the dead, may develop into a "progressive circle" and hold "committee meetings," which spirits will cheerfully attend. There are some weak mortals who cherish a hope that when they are done with life they will also be done with committees; but this is a lethargic frame of mind. Virile and vigorous spirits will bustle throughout eternity. "Wherever Macaulay may be," muses a British satirist, "I am sure he is talking hard, or writing earnestly, for the instruction of his companions."

Every department of spiritism is carefully handled in this painstaking little manual, and much useful advice is given. We are warned against asking "test" questions, which are, for the most part, a waste of time, besides being annoying to a well-bred spirit. Only when great historic figures appear at a séance may we suspect—not a lying medium, but a jest on the part of the merry dead. "There is probably some amusement to be extracted from personating Julius Cæsar, Luther, Napoleon, Disraeli or Gladstone, and inducing both mediums and sitters to accept with reverence the pompous utterances of ridiculous banalities."

Heaven knows we do not begrudge the spirits their little jokes. The unutterable dreariness and futility of their existence (which may perhaps be our existence) lends a sting to death, and victory to the grave. The paralyzing thought that we may one day be lifting table legs, rattling keys or writing misspelled, unpunctuated letters humiliates our souls.

And to what end? The crux of the whole agitating business is expressed in the brief sentence which concludes the "Handbook": "Let us speak to the dead, and let us add their knowledge and counsel to the common store." So far neither knowledge nor counsel has been of much value to the living world. Saul was apparently the only man whom the dead ever enlightened. He at least got a plain answer to a plain question. There has been a lamentable decline in mediums, spirits and controls since the Witch of Endor died.

HOW TO SPEAK
WITH THE DEAD
A PRACTICAL HANDBOOK

By SCIENS

CONTENTS

PREFACE

PRACTICAL instructions for speaking with the dead are given in Chapter VII of this book. Inasmuch, however, as rational men and women do not care to enter upon systematic proceedings of any kind without having some reasonable assurance that a commensurate result will follow, it has been thought desirable to add, in Chapters I to IV, a general outline of the scientific facts and arguments on which the certainties of "survival" and "communication" are based. In Chapters V and VI some necessary information as to mediums and communicating is given. And, in Chapter VIII, the distinction between Speaking with the Dead on the one hand, and Spiritualism faced by Rationalism on the other, is made clear.

The book is strictly impartial from all points of view—whether Religious, Scientific, Agnostic, Spiritualistic, or Rationalistic. It is impersonal. It sets aside the writer's own occult experience which, in the course of a long life devoted mainly to scientific pursuits, has happened to be very considerable. It is a mere cold, neutral text-book. The hard facts of the case are alone responsible for the circumstance that it shows Science to be a sponsor for the reality of speaking with the dead.

A few words—which many persons will read with amazement—must be added here on the subject of *Cui bono?* Multitudinous vials of scorn have been poured out on the inanities of ordinary spiritualistic *séances*; and all research into such matters is rigidly boycotted in scientific circles as being unworthy of any intelligent individual s notice. Even when the President of the Royal Society himself, and others who are entitled to write F.R.S. or D.Sc. after their names, have been known to touch the accursed and degrading thing, they have been either ostracised or half -pardoned contemptuously. This attitude is based on the belief that occultism is an idle and vain form of mental activity, and cannot, with any reason, be expected to add anything to the stock of human knowledge or to produce results of service to mankind. *Cui bono?* Why waste time in tomfoolery that can never be useful and may possibly lead feeble persons into the abyss of insanity?

The defect of the attitude is that it is unscientific. The proudest claim of Science is that she deals with the Facts of the universe and gives her allegiance to Truth rather than to Opinion. But these features are the characteristics of every well-conducted sitting for the development of psychical manifestations. The search is for facts; and the object pursued is the attainment of truth. If, then, a leader of science denounce the sitting as being necessarily futile he does one of two things: either he disallows the proudest claim of Science; or he declares the limits of his own personal knowledge to be those of Fact and Truth.

It has often happened that researches which appeared at the outset to be a mere waste of time have in the end been found productive of much practical and useful knowledge. The modern inquiries into the feasibility of speaking with the dead are a case in point. They have already brought the world of Science and Industry face to face with the possibility and near prospect of a command over Matter and Physical Force such as men have never hitherto enjoyed and such as must lead inevitably to the greatest advance of material prosperity that mankind has ever experienced. This may best be made clear by dealing with some concrete example.

The lessons of the Great War, the utterances of expert authorities like Lord Montagu of Beaulieu, and the newspapers generally, have taught the public that the navigation of the air will be the great and dominating factor of the world's progress in future. This need not be enlarged upon here. Everyone admits that the command of the air will solve the problem of intercourse between all the regions of the globe, and will bring in its train a vast improvement in all the arts of living and a greatly-widened distribution of natural wealth.

Now the whole question of aerial navigation hinges absolutely and completely on that of gravitation. The great desideratum is a weightless (*i.e.*, weightless in effect) aeroplane (with, of course, a virtually weightless crew, virtually weightless passengers, and a virtually weightless cargo) which can move fast or slowly as required, which can come to a stop in the air and which cannot fall. Science and industry are now within measurable distance of such virtually weightless aircraft, thanks to the investigators who have not been deterred by obloquy and ostracism from speaking with the dead.

It is usually assumed in scientific circles that gravity is an unsolved mystery and is entirely beyond the scope of human control in the present state of knowledge. The assumption is well founded if by "knowledge" is meant merely that which is possessed by living human beings and derived solely from normal sources. But if there be, in reality, certain intelligences other than ordinary men and women, they may possibly be better informed with regard to the facts of the universe; and if intelligent communication be feasible as between the better informed personalities and their cousins in this life, it is conceivable that some of the latter may thus acquire information which would otherwise be unattainable. This has actually happened with regard to gravitation. Sir William Crookes more than forty years ago entered into communication with supernormal intelligences and carried out certain laboratory experiments that showed the control and modification of gravity to lie within the compass of human ability when guided by the intelligences in question. And many more experiences of a similar or of an analogous kind are on record. The facts are well established and cannot be successfully denied or explained away.

More recent researches have led to some elucidation of the knowledge at which discarnate spirits have arrived with regard to gravitation. They hold that human science is crippled needlessly by its non-recognition of Motion as being in itself an entity distinct from Mass. They hold that Matter is just as much a compound of Mass and Motion as common salt is a compound of sodium and chlorine. They contend further that gravitation is due to the fact that Motion, like heat, may, where human observation is concerned, exist in either a latent or a sensible form; and they assert the practicability of adding to or subtracting from the quantity of Motion in any given bulk of Matter. In proof of the truth of this assertion they point to the phenomena of what is, by psychical enquirers, called "levitation"—phenomena which have been observed and recorded over and over again and may be seen by any person who takes the trouble to attend even an ordinary table-sitting. And they occasionally rally the human personalities with whom they are communicating upon the dullness of apprehension which has hitherto stood in the way of a broad induction from the myriad everyday facts of weight, coiled springs, drawn bows, artificial jumping frogs, jacks-in-boxes, closely touching billiard-balls in a row, projectiles at the moment of terminating their upward flight, cricket-balls at the moment of meeting the stroke of the bat, and all other examples of latent and sensible Motion.

These views entertained by spirits who have been spoken to on the subject have of late been borne out very markedly by Dr. Crawford's experiments, referred to in Chapter I of the present book. Dr. Crawford himself seems to be regarding his tests from the point of view of Mass alone and to be thinking that he is on the track of a new kind of Matter; but his results fit in still better with the long-established facts of levitation and with the new doctrine of Motion that is fast being accepted in Progressive Circles. It is difficult to believe that a living woman can be deprived of a considerable portion of her Mass without sustaining serious physiological injury. It is also difficult to believe that the removed Mass when laid on the floor or on the drawing-board can be invisible. But there is not any difficulty at all in supposing Motion to have been removed from the medium, the chair, the drawing-board and the platform, without any change of either visibility or appearance in any of the entities concerned. When water at 70° Fahr. is cooled down to 50° Fahr. it loses a something we call heat, but the human eye cannot detect any difference in the liquid. When a bowled cricket ball is arrested by the bat it loses a something we call sensible motion, but its outward appearance remains unvaried. We need not therefore expect a human body or a chair to look otherwise than as usual simply because it loses some or all of its latent Motion.

That the knowledge here discussed may be applied practically and that material substances may thus be rendered weightless and so removed from the influence of gravitation is not a mere theory. It is an actual fact: levitation occurs. What now remains to be done is to harness the acquired knowledge and experience into the service of aerial navigation. Certain Progressive Circles are at work. Whether success will be achieved first by Dr. Crawford in his Goligher laboratory, or by Mr. Edison in his "spook factory" where the workmen agree to become recluses for a period of many months, or by the capable director of the still more mysterious establishments in Florence where many a medium has been passed under review during the last two years, or by, haply, some other investigator of whom the present writer has not yet heard, is a matter that must for the time being be allowed to rest on the knees of the gods. What has already been accomplished in public and the remarkable advances now taking place privately are a sufficient answer to the question Cut bono? Speaking with the dead is a practice that is proving of benefit to England and the world at large.

SCIENS.

HOW TO SPEAK WITH
THE DEAD

CHAPTER I

DO THE DEAD STILL LIVE?

IF survival after what is called "death" be not a fact, the idea of communication with the dead becomes nonsensical. The first question, therefore, that has to be asked in any consideration of the subject is—Do the Dead still live? This enquiry may be addressed both to Religion and to Science; and in both cases it will be found that an affirmative reply is given.

So far as Religion is concerned the case is simple enough. It is a matter of common knowledge that nearly all the inhabitants of the world, including a great majority of its scientific men, accept and profess some form of religion. It is also a matter of common knowledge that all religions teach the doctrine of survival; that is to say, they teach that in every individual human being there exists a soul which becomes separated from the body at death and continues to live on in some form of existence while the body decays. The belief, accordingly, of the great majority of mankind is now, and always has been in historical times, that the answer "Yes" must be given to the question—Do the Dead still live?

This is a hard fact that cannot be glossed over or explained away. Where a belief is practically universal reasonable men may well infer that it is not altogether unfounded. Such an inference, however, falls a good deal short of actual proof; and when Religion is asked to supply such proof the response, though satisfactory enough to religious believers, is not acceptable from a scientific point of view. The Bible, for example, and the sacred books of religions other than the Jewish and Christian faiths, contain an abundance of testimony to show that life after death is a reality; and history in general, both ecclesiastical and secular, narrates many occurrences of such survival. The body of evidence thus available is equal in quantity and quality to that which is commonly accepted as sufficient to establish historical facts in general or cases in the law-courts in particular.

But Science asks for something more than human testimony and records. It turns from fallible men to infallible Nature. The only truths which it will accept as proven are those revealed by the senses, by physical observations and by actual experience. It demands also that every truth thus established shall be capable of confirmation by repeated experimental tests. What, therefore, has to be considered in this chapter is whether survival after death is admitted by Science to be one of Nature's truths.

Such an admission has already been made by many of the foremost leaders of Science in both past and present times. Sir Isaac Newton, Faraday, Wallace, Crookes, Lodge, Barrett and other Fellows of the Royal Society were, or are, survivalists. Their judgment of the case is not to be lightly regarded; and by many reasonable men it is looked upon as conclusive. It is, however, assumed that the readers of these pages will not be content to have the matter settled by mere authority, even of the highest degree of eminence; and as scientific men still exist who declare in lectures, speeches and books that the doctrine of survival is a mistaken one, it becomes necessary to make the case clear by an appeal to fully recognised facts that no one, whether survivalist or non-survivalist, can dispute.

The first of these facts is that Science admits the existence of living individual personalities. When a man is made a Fellow of the Royal Society, or when a President of the British Association for the Advancement of Science is elected, the choice falls upon more than a mere bulk of matter combined with a certain amount of force and energy. Added to these there is a something characterised by knowledge, memory, consciousness, will, conscience, morality, a perception of good and evil, a capability of love and hatred, and all the other qualities that go to the making up of what people mean when they speak of a "soul." If "non-survivalists" prefer to use some other word, well and good. Disputes about names are a mere beating of the air. What is of moment is that all parties are agreed as to the real existence of the something to which reference has here been made.

The second fact is that Science admits the "soul" and body of a human being to be distinct and separate entities, even though they may be closely associated. This is not so clearly obvious as the first fact; and some—though not many—scientists may feel disposed to challenge the accuracy of the assertion. It is necessary, therefore, to substantiate it in a detailed fashion.

It is a matter of common knowledge that if a man's

body be deprived of an arm, a leg, an eye, etc., the "soul" is not affected thereby in any essential way. Our hair may be shaved off, our nails cut, our teeth extracted, and our "souls" are none the worse for the operations. A lung may be put out of action by tuberculosis and the "soul" lives on unaffected. A human being may be "apparently drowned" or may become entranced. His breathing may cease, his very heart may stop beating. The ordinary bodily mechanism by means of which the "soul" makes its presence known may cease to be operative, and—as actually happens now and again—the individual may be so "dead" in the judgment of physicians that he or she is laid out for burial, aye, and is sometimes buried in real earnest, while all the time the soul is as full of life as ever it was. Every person of education is aware that these are matters of frequent observation and experience. They cannot be denied. They are not consistent with the idea of the existence of the "soul" being limited by the existence of the body.

The case may be put even more strongly. In war it often happens that a man is shot through the arm in such a way that a part of a nerve controlling the muscles of certain fingers is destroyed. The fingers thereupon become paralysed; but when a surgeon fills up the gap in the nerve by inserting a piece of nerve taken freshly from a slaughtered calf the brain finds itself once more able to send its messages to the muscles, and the man finds he can move his fingers. Absolute proof thus exists that the brain and the fingers are distinct and separate entities; and it would be utterly unscientific to infer that the observed paralysis indicates necessarily any disappearance of, or change in, the brain. What really occurs is merely that the brain is deprived, for the time being, of one of the tools it is in the habit of using for the purpose of exercising its authority over the body.

Consider, too, what takes place when a man has a "stroke," as it is termed—an apoplectic fit, the breaking of a small blood-vessel in the brain. The exuded blood forms a clot which presses upon some of the brain-cells and interferes with the normality of their action. In some cases the cells affected are those that influence the organs of speech. The man becomes dumb or cannot pronounce correctly. He has the will to speak in his ordinary manner and he makes desperate efforts to do so. These remain unavailing until the blood-clot becomes absorbed and ceases to interfere with the brain-cells; and then the man's will is once more able to exert its authority over the latter, which, in their turn, are once more able to organise and send forward the desired impulses to the tongue, lips, etc. Absolute proof thus exists that the will and the brain are distinct and separate entities; and it would be utterly unscientific to infer that the observed pressure on, and paralysis of, the brain-cells indicates any disappearance of, or change in, the will.

But the will is comprised in the something that is commonly called the "soul." We see, then, that the existence of the soul and body as distinct and separate entities is admitted by Science and demonstrated by the everyday experience of mankind.

It is desirable, however, to add a word or two respecting a phrase and an idea correlated thereto which have long exercised a mischievous influence in psychics and psychology. The phrase is that "thought may possibly be a secretion of the brain." The idea is that although body and mind (or soul) are separate entities neither of them can exist separately from the other.

To speak of thought as a secretion of the brain is to misuse the word "secretion" and to render it meaningless, in which case the famous phrase becomes nonsensical. A secretion is a material substance organised from, and by, some other, parent, material substance. It belongs to the domain of physics and can be expressed in terms of statics and dynamics. Nothing of all this is possible with regard to thought, which belongs to the domain of metaphysics and is immaterial. To speak of something immaterial being organised from something material is an abuse of language, and reduces discussion to an idle jangle of articulate sounds.

There is not anything similarly nonsensical in the idea of body and soul being interdependent entities. The question is one of simple fact and observation. It is a matter of common knowledge that human bodies continue to exist long after their separation from the something that is called "soul." This continued existence may even be unaccompanied (as in the case of mummies) by ordinary decay, and in some cases may involve a prolongation of partial vitality, such as, for instance, the well-known phenomenon of the growth of hair and nails after "death." But that the soul has ceased to be united as before with the body is, in all cases, a matter of certainty. Hence the idea now being discussed obviously requires amendment. It is not permissible to say that body is perpetually dependent upon soul. And the question remains whether it is permissible to say that the existence of an individual soul is dependent upon its remaining attached to the body it accompanied during life.

This leads to the third of the facts to be considered—the fact, namely, that Science admits the possibility of "souls" continuing to exist when detached from the bodies with which they are usually associated. The word "detached" does not mean necessarily separation by any considerable interval of space, or the complete absence of every means of communication. A man who speaks and a man who hears are spoken of as being detached from each other notwithstanding that they are connected together by a sound-conveying atmosphere. Bricks stacked in a pile are detached separate entities even though, in popular language, they are said to be "touching" one another. So, in the case of a paralysed man, the affected portion of his brain is no longer under the control of his will, and to that extent there's a severance of his body from his soul; while in cases of complete trance the detachment in question extends to the entire material organism, and also to the entire psychical entity. The soul becomes, for the time being, wholly separated from the body, which no longer is actuated by consciousness, sensation, memory, thought or volition. All that serves to distinguish the state of things from "death" is the absence of bodily decomposition, together with one or two other physical peculiarities, such as the response of the muscles to electrical excitement and the ophthalmoscopic appearances of the fundus oculi. Yet, when the trance comes to an end, the normal intimate association of soul and body is resumed, and both soul and body are found to be unchanged.

Now, this is a matter of common knowledge among educated persons and has often been made a subject of scientific observation. It proves, clearly enough, that souls can exist independently of material bodies; and the proof will not be disputed by any man of science who is concerned to speak of things as they are, and who uses words in their ordinary plain meaning and not for the purpose of dialectical subtleties.

Trance, however, is not the only form of separate soul-existence that comes within the range of human experience, A very much more common occurrence is that of sleep. Here the scientist will hesitate a little before making any admission. The view now taken by Science of sleep is that the phenomenon is "a natural condition of insensibility, more or less complete, recurring normally (for the adult) with each night," and further, that "the cause of sleep is undetermined, but is supposed to depend upon the production of sedative agents during our waking activities which ultimately clog the higher functions of the brain." It is also held that "in natural deep sleep all the higher brain-centres are more or less out of action, together with the senses of sight, touch, taste, smell and hearing, though in varying degrees." And, with regard to dreaming, the explanation given is that "the gradual passing of the higher nerve-centres—i.e. the highest centres of the cerebral matter—from normal to subnormal activity, or rest, removes from the lower centres a certain inhibition, and these respond more readily both to external stimuli and to altered internal stimuli or tension of the blood-vessels. Accompanying this functional dissolution of the higher centres there is, in varying degrees, dissociation of consciousness or obstructed association. . . . The result of such dissociation is interference with judgment, resulting in false perception, illusion, hallucination and perpetually altering variations of these."

What is meant by the phrase "dissociation of consciousness"? It cannot very well signify anything other than that consciousness during sleep becomes detached from the brain, sometimes to a partial extent and some-times completely. This is the same thing as saying that soul is found by universal experience to exist, time and again, in a state of independence. To that extent the scientific view is well-founded and acceptable. When, however, dreams are stated to be nothing more than mere physical states of the lower brain-centres a doubt creeps in. Dreams are not material. They are intangible thoughts and belong to the domain of conscious-ness. Where the "removal of a certain inhibition from the lower centres" comes in is by way of explaining that owing to temporary physical conditions attending sleep, various brain-cells are out of gear, as it were, and work irregularly—the case being analogous to that of the man who is dumb or speaks badly owing to a blood-clot in his brain. But at the back of the fantastic or imperfect ap-pearance are the Consciousness and other elements of the soul marshalled in regular co-ordination. It is more probable, therefore, that dreams are distortions of re-alities perceived by the soul than that they originate in disordered cerebral matter.

We see, then, that Science is faced by, and admits, three fundamental facts, namely—

1. The existence, in this world, of human souls as well as human bodies.
2. The existence of such souls and bodies as separate entities,
3. The possibility of souls continuing to exist when separated from human bodies.

What has next to be considered is whether such separate existence is limited to the case of temporary detachment during the life of the body, or whether it is also possible when the separation is brought about by "death."

Reasoning by analogy may not be tantamount to direct proof; but it is, none the less, cogent. When we reflect that the loss of an arm, a leg, etc., is really the happening of death to the missing parts of the body and yet that the soul is not thereby affected we are entitled to infer that the loss of the rest of the body will leave the soul unscathed. And when we add the reflection that in cases of trance, apparent drowning, deep sleep, etc., the whole body is detached from the soul—a separation that occasionally lasts many days or weeks—the inference is greatly strengthened. Everyone knows, moreover, that in many instances of natural death the soul remains in vigorous existence right up to the moment of dissolution; and where death occurs from external causes, as in warfare, both body and soul maintain their full normality until the stroke of Fate has been dealt. Why, then, should it be assumed that the soul ceases suddenly to exist? The body is seen to continue, and, as regards its matter, to be imperishable. The soul is not seen; but as it never had been seen, though known to exist, during life, no reason can be assigned for expecting it to be visible at death. Not even the flimsiest foundation can be discovered for the doctrine of non-survival, which is merely the arbitrary assertion of a most patent improbability. It is, therefore, unscientific in the highest degree.

In addition, however, to this analogical argument, which most scientific men regard as conclusive, there exists a solid basis of scientifically observed facts demonstrating very clearly the survival of souls after death. The facts, it is true, are psychical rather than physical;

but this does not impair their validity. Modern men of science are beginning to regard matter, force and energy as less important in the scheme of the universe than are the entities that cannot be expressed in dynamical terms; and the biologists are fast conceding priority to will and conscious purpose over the hitherto accepted supreme authority of Evolutionary Life. Still, the observations above alluded to are in part of a physical character and have been made within the sacred precincts of scientific laboratories.

Dealing first with the latter, it suffices, by way of example, to mention the researches conducted by Mr. W. J. Crawford, D.Sc, a gentleman who is Lecturer in Mechanical Engineering in the Belfast Municipal Technical Institute, Extra-Mural Lecturer in Mechanical Engineering in the Queen's University of Belfast, etc. It is a matter of common knowledge in scientific circles, and to a large extent in popular circles as well, that he has, with respect to the "survival" question, carried out a series of experiments and tests under the most rigid conditions for ensuring accuracy of observation and correctness of results—experiments and tests that have been witnessed by competent persons and carefully recorded in a manner to which no valid exception can be taken. In the ordinary way of scientific work the conclusions arrived at by such a trained and eminently well-qualified observer would be assented to by the scientific world as a matter of course; and such assent should not be withheld merely because the field of investigation lay outside the beaten tracks of Science.

Dr. Crawford's observations and experiments are of quite recent date. They have impressed greatly the scientific world. They are regarded as proving the existence of the "invisible intelligent beings" mentioned by Sir William Crookes in 1874, and as also proving that these beings are encountered and communicated with here in this world. But the knowledge of the work done by Dr. Crawford is not yet very widely spread, and it is quite possible that many scientific men as well as a good portion of the public at large are still unacquainted with its character and the results attained. It may be well, therefore, to cite an illustrative instance of one of the methods employed. This is done in the scientist's own words:—

"A drawing-board was placed on the platform of a weighing-machine and a chair was placed on the top of the board. The medium (Miss Goligher) sat on the chair, with her feet resting on the board.

"*Experiment* 1. — I said to the operators [*i.e.* to the spirits], 'You say the levitating cantilever contains matter from the body of the medium. I want you to take out from her body the matter you use in the construction of the cantilever you employ to levitate this table (weight 12 1/4 lbs.) and to place this matter loosely on the floor—not to build up the cantilever but simply to place the matter required for it on the floor. Give three raps when you have done this.'

"The medium's weight began to decrease and in a few seconds became fairly steady. Then I heard the three raps, signifying that the operation was complete.

RESULT:

Weight of medium + chair + board,
      before the experiment . . . . 9 st. 12 1/2 lbs.

Fairly steady weight of medium + chair + board,

   after the raps were given   . . . .   8 st. 10 1/2 lbs.

Decrease in weight of medium   . . . .   0 st. 16 lbs.

   "It is noteworthy that when I carried out the same test about eighteen months previously, I obtained the same result within a pound or two.

   "*Experiment* 2.—I asked the operators to put the matter they said they abstracted in Experiment 1, not on the floor but on the drawing-board under the medium's chair (the drawing-board was resting on the platform of the weighing-machine). They gave three raps when the operation was complete.

RESULT:

   "The medium's weight showed no difference from her normal of 9 st. 12 1/2 lbs.

   "This, of course, is as it should be, as any actual matter taken from her body and placed on the drawing-board would still be accounted for by the weighing-machine, provided that such matter was acted upon by gravity in the normal way."

   Here, as is obvious, was a laboratory experiment of the simplest nature and not open to any doubt or cavil. It was a mere weighing operation to determine whether any loss of weight took place in the material objects on the platform of the machine. The medium, as a person, did not enter into the problem at all. It was not a question of her good faith any more than it was the question of the good faith of the chair or the drawing-board. Nor was it the case of a phenomenon occurring in darkness or under conditions that rendered close observation difficult; while, as for Dr. Crawford himself, it will not be contended that he was incompetent to read the indications of the machine or to report them correctly. Yet his spoken instructions to something invisible and intangible were followed by results that indicated intelligent hearing and careful obedience. To deny that this was strict scientific proof of the presence in Dr. Crawford's laboratory of some kind of consciousness, perception and will—i.e. of some "soul"—that was separate and distinct from any soul in normal association with a human body would be to speak as perversely as though one were to deny that two and two make four.

So much for the physical category of the observations that have been made in the scientific world respecting survival after death. We can now turn to the psychical category.

The investigations in this direction have been carried on for so many years and by so many observers, both scientific and lay, that a vast mass of material has accumulated in the shape of evidence which, for the greater part, is in favour of an affirmative answer being given to the question—Do the Dead still live? None of the evidence is, in fact, suggestive of a negative reply; but some is not of a trustworthy character, while in other cases the requisite corroboration is lacking. This is a trap for the unwary of both schools of thought—the sceptical and the credulous. The former are struck by instances of fraud, deceit and ignorant gullibility; and they neglect to consider and weigh what is brought forward of a serious and genuine character. The latter are carried away by their emotions and wishes, and prefer the sensational rubbish to the calm and balanced testimony of honest and careful observers.

A typical collection of the evidence here referred to—good, bad and indifferent—is to be found in the pages of "Raymond," the recently published book written by Sir Oliver Lodge, F.R.S. The author, who has for very many years been an eminent investigator of psychical phenomena, in addition to having attained the highest rank in the scientific world in respect of his electrical and other work, was afflicted by the loss of a son, Raymond, in the Great War, and, in accordance with what he considered to be possible, he endeavoured to open up communication with the discarnate spirit of the deceased young man. He describes his experiments and their result in the book he has written. He does not hesitate to reject much of what he observed as being "nonsense," and a good deal more he describes as "unverifiable" and doubtful. But he also brings forward an abundance of what he terms "evidential matter," which he deems to be genuine and convincing—a conclusion fully accepted by serious readers who are not swayed by prejudice. He makes many references to what has been done by other investigators, and he expresses himself on the general question as follows: —

"However it be accomplished, and whatever reception the present-day scientific world may give to the assertion, there are many now who know, by first-hand experience, that communication is possible across the boundary—if there is a boundary—between the world apprehended by our few animal-derived senses and the larger existence concerning which our knowledge is still more limited. Communication is not easy, but it occurs. . . . The more recent development of an elaborate scheme of cross-correspondence entered upon since the death of specially experienced and critical investigators of the Society for Psychical Research, who were familiar with all these difficulties, and who have taken strong and most ingenious means to overcome them, has made the proof, already very strong, now almost crucial. . . . The chief thing that the episode establishes, to my mind, and a thing that was worth establishing, is the genuine character of the simple domestic sittings, without a medium, which are occasionally held by the family circle at Mariemont. For it is through these chiefly that Raymond remains as much a member of the family group as ever. ... In the old days, if I sat with a medium, I was never told of any serious imaginary bereavement which had befallen myself — beyond the natural and inevitable losses from an older generation which fall to the lot of every son of man. But now if I, or any member of my family, goes anonymously to a genuine medium, giving not the slightest normal clue, my son is quickly to the fore and continues his clear and convincing series of evidences; sometimes giving testimony of a critically selected kind, sometimes contenting himself with friendly family chaff and reminiscences, but always acting in a manner consistent with his personality and memories and varying moods. ... In every way he has shown himself anxious to give convincing evidence. Moreover, he wants me to speak out; and I shall. I am as convinced of continued existence, on the other side of death, as I am of existence here."

These personal utterances represent much more than the opinion of a single individual. They are in effect a summary of what has been established by the laborious investigations of many hundreds of educated and capable enquirers—including highly-honoured leaders of science—during the last half-century. The Society of Psychical Research, for example—mentioned by Sir Oliver Lodge—comprises, and has comprised, many of the foremost scientists and philosophical thinkers of England, America, France, Italy and other countries. It entered upon the investigation and study of psychical phenomena from a strictly scientific point of view, without any tendency to be guided by religious teachings and desirous of stamping out the influence of so-called Spiritualism upon public credulity. Its work was conducted with the utmost care and caution in every detail. Its Reports from year to year were welcomed as sound and trustworthy textbooks in a little-known region of science. They are collections of demonstrated facts rather than the presentation of inferences and speculative views. So when it is found that the foremost psychologists and psychical investigators work in harmony with the results attained by the Society for Psychical Research, and that the conclusions announced by authorities like Sir Oliver Lodge are largely based upon such results, the case for the acceptance of these conclusions becomes very strong indeed.

It has now been proved beyond all possibility of reasonable refutation that both Religion and Science answer "Yes" when they are asked the question—Do the Dead still live?

There is an allied question which should not be altogether ignored. Euclid sometimes proves a proposition by showing that its denial necessarily involves an absurdity. In like manner we may ask whether the denial of the proposition that souls live on after death drives us into a position that the common sense and conscience of mankind know to be untenable.

If this life be the whole measure of the existence of a soul, if birth mean its beginning and death its end, the something that is called "soul" is seen to be merely a temporary evanescent affection of the matter that constitutes the body. But it is an abuse of language to speak of matter as being either morally good or morally bad. Even if it be admitted that matter can live and be endowed with consciousness and volition, there would still be a manifest absurdity in attributing to it a knowledge of good and evil. It follows, therefore, that any person who is a thorough-going materialist is logically debarred from speaking of goodness, benevolence, honour, integrity, charity, truth, piety, patriotism, profligacy, fraud, crime or wickedness. The masses of matter to which he gives the name "human beings" are non-moral just as much as his table or his boots. He talks nonsense when he praises them for acting in a manner which he calls "right," or when he blames them for acting in a manner which he calls "wrong." Nor is the case bettered by conceding that "good conduct" may be beneficial and "bad conduct" harmful to the mass of matter in action, and may therefore* in an analogical way, be described as meriting commendation and reproof respectively. The mass of matter will know well enough that success, prosperity and worldly enjoyment are attained much more frequently by bad men than by the righteous, and he will laugh at the idea of a satisfied conscience being preferred to a satisfied body. He will know that when death comes the good will not be any better off than the bad—they will both be annihilated—and he will also know that during life the bad are much better off than the good. Does this doctrine commend itself to any sane man? Does any leader of science exist who will say deliberately that he repudiates the doctrine of right and wrong? If he will not say this he must not say that souls are merely appurtenances of bodies and cease to exist after death.

CHAPTER II

SOUL AND LIFE

The phrase that the dead still live does not mean the same thing as when it is said that a human body lives. In the former ease the word "live" merely means "exist"; in the latter the word "lives" connotes, together with the idea of existence, a particular concrete form of living which is differentiated markedly from "living" in the abstract. This distinction is frequently overlooked, and as the oversight leads to much confusion of thought and lies at the root of much of the opposition that is here and there offered to the doctrine of "survival," it seems well to devote a few pages to its discussion.

The "life" that is found in human bodies and throughout the organic world is impersonal. It is material, or, rather, physical, in the sense that it has not any existence apart from the organic matter of which it constitutes an affection or attribute. The case is analogous to that of gravitation. According to the accepted Newtonian philosophy every particle of matter in the

universe attracts, and is attracted by, every other particle: it gravitates: it is ponderable. But there is no such
thing as gravitation *per se*, though there may be an entity
that causes gravitation. It is convenient, for the purposes
of language and the orderly expression of thought, to
speak of it separately, just as colour, temperature, illumination, form, structure and other affections are referred
to; the understanding, however, being always that they
are not in themselves entities and are not characterised
by anything in the nature of self-existence.

Science does not at present hold that life is an attribute of all matter. Minerals and other forms of what
is called inorganic matter are considered to be devoid
of life, and the same destitution is asserted with respect to "dead," "inanimate" organic matter. Life is
met with only in "living," "animate" organic matter;
just as crystallisation is found only in "crystalline" and
not in "amorphous" matter; and—to pursue the simi-
le—it may be pointed out that the same matter which is
crystalline under some conditions becomes amorphous
under others, as in the case of carbon, which is sometimes diamond and sometimes charcoal. In like manner
living matter may change into dead matter—a change
which is called "death"; and dead matter may change
into living matter, as, for example, when food is assim-
ilated by animals and vegetables. The true nature of
the "life" met with in living organic matter is not yet
understood. Modern science has shown, indisputably,
that the doctrine of the conservation of energy applies
without modification to living beings just as much as to
inanimate substances. The idea of there being any specific "vital force," "vital material" or "vital energy" has
long ago been abandoned. All the particular phenome-

na observed by morphologists, physiologists, embryolo-
gists, palaeontologists and setiologists—i.e. by the whole
world of biologists—can be satisfactorily explained in
terms of chemistry, physical force, energy and dynamics.
But biology cannot as yet give an equally clear account
of the co-ordinated vitality of anything that lives. It cannot even state the how and why of the simplest unicellu-
lar organism. "We are forced," says a leading authority,
"to the conclusion that a living organism is a particular
synthesis of matter and energy, the secret of whose or-
ganisation remains hidden."

We know, however, that life displays the same kind
of uniformity that characterises heat, light, motion and
other imponderables. The something that appears as
the temperature of boiling water is similar in all respects
to the something that appears as the equal temperature
of hot oil and can be interchanged therewith. Indeed,
the fundamental Theory of Exchanges upon which a
great part of thermodynamics is based depends for its
validity on the absence of any distinction between the
heats of various masses of matter. The only variation of
heat is that of degree: the kind is always the same; heat
never becomes individualised. This is seen by everyday
observation to be equally true of life, and is frequently
demonstrated by specific experiment. Grafting, for example, whether it consist in the union of a scion of one
tree with the stock of another, or whether it take the
form of transferring a piece of John Smith's skin to a
flayed part of Robert Green's arm, is the migration of
a vitality that remains unchanged in spite of the change
of environment and that intermingles harmoniously
and homogeneously with the vitality of its new abode.
Neither the individualities of the two trees nor the per-

sonalities of the two men appear in, or accompany, their stocks of "life" any more than they are to be found in their stocks of heat or weight. The various stocks may be more or less abundant in quantity, but they do not differ in kind.

We know also that life is capable of indefinite increase by reproduction, provided only that the means of sustenance be available. A single pair of rabbits, for instance, if allowed to breed unchecked and not killed off, will, in a comparatively short time, become represented by two millions of similar animals. This means, of course, that the quantity of "life" corresponding to two rabbits has been augmented a million-fold. The increase has not been derived from the food consumed, the total amount of which is accounted for by the bodies and excreta of the conies. A similar phenomenon is observable throughout the whole sum of living beings, whether human, "animal" or vegetable. It distinguishes "life" very effectually from matter and energy, both of which are, by the doctrine of conservation, as incapable of increase as of decrease. The only hypothesis that appears possible by way of explanation is to hold that "life" is one of the protean modes of energy in the same way that heat is understood (by those persons who are content to accept the Baconian, and modern scientific view) to be a mode of motion. This hypothesis, however, does not rest on any secure foundation. The only energy that is known to be practically available for transmutation into life is heat (light and electricity seem to be negligible); and reproduction, which often takes place on a very large scale, has never been observed to involve the absorption and disappearance of heat.

Again, we know by observation and experiment

that the function of "life" is to organise matter; that is
to say, to arrange material particles into differentiated
groups and aggregates marked by varying complexities
of composition suitable for certain specific actions. It is
sometimes contended that this systematic co-ordination
and apparent display of purpose is to be found also in
the inanimate world. The phenomenon of crystallisation, for example, is here and there regarded as an instance of life. It is attended by growth. It exhibits both
differentiation and integration, becoming on the one
hand more complex and on the other more unified. Lost
parts are seen to be regenerated. Some degree of adjust-
ment to surroundings is noticeable; and reproduction
may even be said to occur to some extent. But when the
crystal is formed it does not differ, either in substance or
in function, from the raw material out of which it has
been constructed. It remains inert and destitute of any
approach to vitality. It may be destroyed by crushing,
fusion, solution: it never "dies," To speak of it as being a
living creature is, therefore, inept.

If, however, great importance be still attached to the
(occasional regenerations and reproductions observed
in the case of inanimate matter, it should be borne in
mind that these differ very greatly from the corresponding phenomena where life is concerned. The repairs
effected by chemical affinity and other non-vital influences are limited to restoration and replacement without alteration of structure or change of adaptation; and
where reproduction takes place it is limited to repetition.
Very different results are met with when Life is in control. Take any "horny-handed son of toil." The skin of
his hands when he was a child and until he began to
work was soft and tender. It became injured by friction,

pressure and the like. It needed repair; and then Life, instead of renewing the softness, gradually developed a condition of toughness and callosity which served as a safeguard against further injury. Such facts as these—and a vast number are known to Science—conclusively establish the essential difference that exists between living matter and matter that is not invested with vitality. Then, too, we know that Life is not characterised by consciousness. This is clearly evident in the cases of seeds and eggs which are most assuredly composed of living matter. But it is also just as obvious in fully matured human beings if careful consideration be given to all the facts involved. A man's bones, for example, are endowed with life; but no one suggests or contends that they are characterised by consciousness. The same thing is true of his hair, his nails, his flesh, his blood. His eyes and ears and other organs of sense are mere receiving and transmitting apparatus, and are not in themselves conscious. Hence by far the greater part of the life that enters into the composition of a living human being is devoid of consciousness. And when the brain is taken into account the situation is not changed. Cerebral matter is, like the sensory mechanism, a mere piece of apparatus, a gramophone, as it were, which, in a certain sense of the words, may be said to hear and to speak, but which has not any inner consciousness of what goes on. This view, which no man of science will contest, and which is a tenet of modern natural philosophy, is established by the everyday experience of every man. Not only does he know that his bones, hair, blood, etc., are not conscious entities,) though they are full of life; he also knows that he remains as alive as ever during his sleep, which is frequently dreamless and free from all indications of consciousness. He knows that chloro-form and other anaesthetics are constantly employed on thousands of occasions with resulting insensibility and unconsciousness, but with no difference in the life that animates the bodies of the persons operated upon. He knows that a man may be stunned by a severe blow on the head and may become, for the time being, bereft of consciousness while still retaining his full vitality. The truth of the matter, in fact, is so plain as not to be open to any serious discussion, even though, as is the case with every doctrine under the sun, it may in appearance be argued about in words and phrases that are ingeniously diverted from their normal meanings.

It is furthermore to be borne in mind that Life has not any conscience and is utterly non-moral. From a strictly scientific point of view this is not a matter of any consequence; for Science is concerned merely with existence qua existence and disregards the whole subject of ethical good and evil. Scientific men, however, have consciences and the knowledge of right and wrong, and are able, whenever they may feel so disposed, to judge of Life from the moral point of view. They see, for example, that the vitality of a living human being is just as active, efficient and exquisitely adaptative in the development of a painful disease as in the production of enjoyable health. They see that the fatal microbe is fostered and

LIFE	SOUL
1. Is impersonal. It has not any individualities or idiosyncrasies.	1. Is personal. Individual souls exist as separate entities and each has its own distinguishing character.

LIFE *(continued)*

SOUL *(continued)*

2. Is homogeneous. It is divisible into separate portions only in the same sense that the same is true of heat, light, electricity, and other forms of physical energy. These various parcels coalesce when brought into contact with each other and form a whole that is uniform without any differentiation.

2. Is heterogeneous. Souls are distinct from each other and do not coalesce.

3. Is the organiser of matter and the controlling influence that determines the morphology, physiology, embryology, palaeontology and aetiology of the organisms produced.

3. Is the employer of the organs formed by Life.

4. Is non-conscious, non-sensory and incapable of thought or memory.

4. Is conscious, perceptive, sensitive, emotional, intelligent, thinking, and mnemonic.

5. Is non-moral. It is conscienceless without any knowledge of good and evil. Its functions are

5. Is characterised by volition, accompanied by a full understanding of good and evil. It is capa-

performed mechanically without any regard to what results may ensue.

6. Is capable of indefinite increase by reproduction. It may possibly be originated by a particular grouping of material atoms in combination with particular physical forces and under particular physical conditions.

ble of acting rightly and wrongly and of appreciating the results of its actions.

6. Is incapable of reproduction. Each individual soul is a self-contained, self-sufficing, self-continuing entity that has not originated from any other soul or from any matter of physical force.

sent on its murderous way rejoicing, just as much as the phagocytes (the "blood scavengers") and other defensive organisms are in like manner protected and caused to multiply. The cow is made to yield milk, while the cobra is equally aided to prepare a store of deadly poison. The bee is set to the beneficent work of honey-making; and the mosquito is granted a letter-of-marque for the dissemination of malaria. Everywhere in nature the same blindness to moral considerations and the same absence of ethical purpose are met with in the activities of Life.

The question of how Life originates should also receive attention. Modern science rejects the idea of its being derived from inanimate matter or from any combination of matter with physical force or energy. The experiments of the late Dr. H. Charlton Bastian, F.R.S., and others with respect to the demonstration of "spontaneous generation" are held to be invalidated by various sources of error; and the almost unanimous verdict of the scientific world is that every occurrence of life proceeds from some antecedent, parent, life. This doctrine involves naturally the referring back of the entire amount of life now existing in the world to a long line of ancestry. And as Science teaches furthermore that a time did once exist when the world was altogether inorganic and inanimate, there emerges the problem of when and how Life made its first appearance on this mundane sphere. This problem is, as yet, insoluble; and, faute de mieux, certain scientists as, for example, Helmholz, Tyndall and Lord Kelvin have found themselves reduced to the necessity of suggesting that possibly the first specimen of life on the earth was introduced in the form of some organism borne hither by a meteorite. But such a suggestion does not solve the problem of Life; it merely throws back the solution by yet another stage. And in the meantime the remarks already made in the present chapter with regard to the capacity of indefinite increase displayed by Life are emphasised and confirmed in a prodigious degree. It is surely a most marvellous thing that the whole vast volume of existing life should be the product of some minute primordial quantity without there ever having been added any growth-material from the outside. This difficulty was felt by Dr. Bastian and his fellow-experimenters; and even the stoutest upholders of Harvey's doctrine, omne vivum ex ovo, as, for instance, Huxley, Haeckel, Nageli, Pflüger and Ray Lankester have not hesitated to admit the possibility of protoplasm having been synthetically derived from inanimate matter at some early period of the earth's history, when physical conditions were very different from those of the present time and when so many things were "in the making." Some scientists, indeed, hold that heterogenesis may even now be taking place in localities or under circumstances that are shielded from observation; and others, basing their judgment upon the triumphs of modern chemistry in the synthesis of sugar, indigo, alizarine, urea and other organic substances, think it probable that men may yet succeed in putting together a combination of matter that shall exhibit vitality as one of its attributes. The bearing of all this upon the problems dealt with in the present volume consists, of course, in the support given to the essentially physical and non-psychical nature of Life.

If a comparison be now made between what has here been stated with regard to Life and what was stated in Chapter I with regard to Soul, we shall find ourselves in presence of certain marked contrasts as follows:

These contrasts necessitate a duality of signification of the word "death." When the death of an organic being is spoken of, the phrase implies that the matter of which it is composed has lost its attribute of vitality (an analogous case being the reduction of the temperature of a body to absolute zero). And where the organic being is a member of the human race (the question of the souls of animals and vegetables does not lie within the scope of this book) the phrase also implies that the soul and body have become separated so completely as to terminate the employment of the latter by the former.

The very pith of the arguments that are sometimes advanced against the idea of "survival" is to be found in this double meaning of the word "death." When the belief is asserted that "death is the end" and that there is not any "future life," the statements are reasonable and well-founded if regard be had solely to the phenomena of Life and to the relations of Life with the body. The knight who contended that the shield was of silver maintained a true enough view; as also did the knight who advanced from the opposite direction and, having seen the other side of the suspended buckler, declared it to be of gold. Death is continued death so far as the question of physical Life is concerned: it is merely a change of stage in psychical existence.

CHAPTER III

TELEPATHY AND TELE-MNEMONIKY

SCIENCE has not yet accepted definitely the existence of telepathy and can hardly be said to have even begun the study of tele-mnemoniky. But the idea of these matters is so intermingled with the subjects of "survivals" and "communications," and—as regards telepathy at least—appears so frequently in psychical literature, that it is desirable for those who contemplate speaking with the dead to become acquainted with the general nature of the problems and facts involved therein.

Many people are aware—and, indeed, have themselves tried the experiment—that mind can influence mind without the intervention of matter, such as the organs of speech and hearing operating in a sound-conveying atmosphere, A common phenomenon is the mental impression of a person being present who has approached without being seen or heard. A somewhat less frequent, but still sufficiently familiar, instance of the same order of things is to be found in the fact that persons who are looked at intently (even behind their backs) often become uneasy and turn to meet the gaze. So, also, it is found that cases occur of persons suddenly, and without any apparent cause, finding themselves thinking earnestly of certain other persons and learning subsequently that those other persons were at, or a little before, the time of the impression thinking of the persons impressed.

Facts such as these—which are positive and undisputed—have led to experimental tests, conducted scientifically, for the purpose of determining whether it is possible, at will, to establish intelligent communications between transmitters and percipients who are at a distance from each other; and the name "telepathy" has been given to the kind of intercourse in question. The work has been conducted chiefly by the Society for Psychical Research, whose Reports on the subject have become classics. Telepathy is recognised in so far as it is a grouping of observed facts; but it has not hitherto advanced beyond the status of a "working hypothesis," which, however, still awaits precise formulation. Thus, Sir Oliver Lodge, F.R.S., in his "Raymond" first published in November, 1916, says—

"The fact of telepathy proves that bodily organs are not absolutely essential to communication of ideas. Mind turns out to be able to act directly on mind, and stimulate it into response by other than material means. Thought does not belong to the material region, although it is able to exert an influence on that region through mechanism provided by vitality. Yet the means whereby it accomplishes the feat are essentially unknown, and the fact that such interaction is possible would be strange and surprising if we were not too much accustomed to it. It is reasonable to suppose that the mind can be more at home, and more directly and more exuberantly active, when the need for such interaction between psychical and physical—or let us more safely and specifically say between mental and material—no longer exists, when the restraining influence of brain and nerve mechanism is removed, and when some of the limitations connected with bodily location in space are ended.

"Experience must be our guide. To shut the door on actual observation and experiment in this particular region, because of preconceived ideas and obstinate prejudice, is an attitude common enough, even among scientific men; but it is an attitude markedly unscientific. Certain people have decided that inquiry into the activities of discarnate mind is futile; some few consider it impious; many, perhaps wisely distrusting their own powers, shrink from entering on such an inquiry. But if there are any facts to be ascertained, it must be the duty of some volunteers to ascertain them: and for people having any acquaintance with scientific history to shut their eyes to facts when definitely announced, and to forbid investigation or report concerning them on pain of ostracism,—is to imitate a byegone theological attitude in a spirit of unintended flattery—a flattery which from every point of view is eccentric; and like-wise to display an extraordinary lack of humour."

It must, however, be added that, a little further on in the same book, Sir Oliver speaks somewhat less positively. He says —

"Matter is an indirect medium of communication between mind and mind. That direct telepathic intercourse should be able to occur between, mind and mind, without all this intermediate physical mechanism, is therefore not really surprising. It has to be proved, no doubt , but the fact is intrinsically less puzzling than many of those other facts to which we have grown hardened by usage."

This account of telepathy is vague, and a similar vagueness also characterises the utterances of other authorities on the same subject. But no good reason exists why the matter should not be dealt with in a manner very much more clear and precise.

We should consider, in the first place, that the word "mind" really means "soul," and is used merely for the sake of convenience as concentrating attention upon the soul's faculty of intelligence apart from its sentient, emotional, volitional and ethical attributes. Accordingly, when a telepathist speaks of mind communicating directly with mind, it is the same thing as saying that soul communicates directly with soul; and this, in its turn, implies the corollary that, whether spirits be incarnate or discarnate, the idea of telepathic intercourse is admissible.

In the next place, it is to be borne in mind that, as shown in Chapter I of this book, every soul has always some definite location in space. Nothing certain is known as to whether the shape and volume of a soul correspond exactly in form and size with those of the human body that is associated with the soul during life on earth. It is sometimes thought, in a speculative way, that the soul extends beyond the confines of the body, which thus becomes invested with an "aura," as it is termed, and can come into contact with other souls even when the respective bodies are more or less apart in space; but no facts have been observed that give serious support to this view. The probabilities, indeed, are in favour of the something—which may or may not be akin to ordinary physical matter—that constitutes a soul having a volume approximating to the space occupied by its earthly body.

A third fundamental consideration is that the actual experiences of every day consist in a large measure of the most astounding instances of communication between widely separated bodies—or bulks of matter—and souls. The sun is distant some 93,000,000 miles from the earth, and yet it can impart sensations of illumination and warmth to a soul on the earth's surface, to say nothing of more subtle influences conveyed by what are known as "dark rays." The fact is indisputable, but it is not yet clearly understood. Physicists have felt themselves compelled to form the hypothesis of an "Ether" pervading interstellar space and serving as a medium or vehicle for the passage of radiant energy from place to place. This Ether has to be conceived of as possessing a nature and attributes quite as wonderful and incomprehensible as anything narrated in the "Arabian Nights" or set forth in the Church doctrine of the Holy Trinity. It is understood to be the means by which the marvels of wireless telegraphy become possible, by which glances are exchanged between human eyes, by which newspapers are read, and by which an artillery observer at the front becomes aware whether the gunners are or are not hitting their mark. Yet there is not any certainty that the particular Ether imagined by modern science exists at all. For anything that is known and proved the medium of communication may in the end turn out to be something quite different. When, therefore, telepathy is spoken of, no scientific man is entitled to reject the idea merely because it involves the existence of some as yet unknown means of interaction. If the fact of telepathy be established he must accept it, even though it may be as yet inexplicable. The knowledge possessed by Science from time to time does not set limits to the realities of the universe.

A soul that formulates a thought is obviously not in quite the same state as was the case before the occurrence of the thought; and if there be in existence some kind of space-filling "X," corresponding to the imagined "Ether" it is conceivable that this change of state may affect or disturb the X in a way analogous to the supposed affecting of the Ether by a change of temperature in a heat-emitting substance. In like manner if some other soul located elsewhere be in contact with the X, it is conceivable that the disturbance of the latter may cause such other soul to experience a corresponding change of state and thus to become impressed with, as it were, a facsimile of the original thought. The myriad complexities of the supposed changes of state and disturbances involved in the communication of a train of thought need not be regarded as an insuperable difficulty. Let anyone study what takes place in the course of a telephonic message. A disk of sheet-iron is caused to vibrate by the air-shaking human voice: these vibrations cause corresponding fluctuations in the electric current flowing through the wire uniting the transmitter with the receiver; and the varying current sets up varying magnetic impulses which cause the receiving disk of sheet-iron to vibrate in a manner exactly similar to what happened in the case of the transmitting disk, so that the air impinging on the listening ear is shaken in the same way as the air affected by the original speaker's voice. It all seems simple enough until the character of the "vibrations" and "fluctuations" is looked into. They are so varied, complex and multitudinous as to defy analysis or even comprehension. The human mind desists from the attempt to really understand them. But telephony remains an acknowledged fact; and its existence lends a high degree of probability to the reality of telepathy.

The term "thought-reading" is often employed to indicate telepathic communication, and is very convenient by reason of its association with what is understood by the common action of perusal. In so-called "spiritualistic sittings" a medium sometimes mentions a name or a circumstance known only to the sitter; and this is frequently considered to be a complete proof of information derived by the medium from some spirit. But it may just as well be a case of thought-reading. The sitter's soul, thinking of the name or circumstance, disturbs the X accordingly. The medium's soul, which is in contact with the X, is affected by the disturbance and becomes conscious of the name or circumstance. In simpler, less cumbrous language, the medium reads the sitter's thoughts.

It is not, however, merely a question of "mediums." Telepathy is important throughout the whole range of communication with the spirit-world. Whenever and wherever a soul—whether still invested with a human body or discarnate—is thinking, it is affecting the X and thereby rendering it possible for other souls to be impressed with the thoughts. For the most part the phenomena are of so faint a character and the minds to be communicated with so "untuned" that the incipient telepathy remains unnoticed and disregarded; but occasionally it commands attention. This view of the case is borne out by ample evidence. Second-sight, dreams, presentiments, "inspiration," and such mental impulses as are commonly considered inexplicable are undoubted facts that fall within the scope of telepathy. In saying this it is not asserted that the phenomena in question are always real. They are frequently delusions due to an overwrought nervous system, to cerebral disorder or to emotional disturbance; but in other cases they are as actual and genuine as the common occurrences of human life. Turning, now, to tele-mnemoniky, or "memory-reading" it is to be remarked that although everyone is familiar with the fact that memory exists, and though everyone quite understands the signification of the word, no one as yet has succeeded in giving even a rudimentary explanation of the faculty of remembrance. The most eminent psychologists have found the matter to be quite beyond the limits of their understanding; as indeed is essentially the case with every faculty of the soul, and—it may be added—with every attribute of matter. The old saying remains as true as ever: "A child can ask questions which a wise man cannot answer."

For practical purposes, however, partial knowledge suffices. Thus the existence of memory as a faculty of the soul is known, and it is also known that this implies the possession by each soul of a store of information. Whatever may be the nature of the storehouse, the doors can be opened and the information set free or rendered subject to inspection. It is conceivable, therefore, that a soul other than the memory-owner may under certain unknown conditions have access to the store.

This is what is meant by tele-mnemoniky—the state of things that exists when not only current thoughts but also the accumulated knowledge resulting from past experience and observation are read by some outside soul. And as every memory contains much that is "pigeon-holed" and out of use for the time being, a very notable result is occasionally met with. Information is elicited as to facts and circumstances of which the person subjected to tele-mnemoniky is no longer conscious; and he, or she, becomes firmly and genuinely convinced that the particulars mentioned must have been derived from some supernormal source.

A word remains to be said regarding the speed of communication in telepathy and tele-mnemoniky. Many persons hesitate to credit the reports of experiments showing that two persons at a considerable distance from each other—located, say, in London and Manchester respectively—are able to exchange thoughts without any appreciable delay. When, however, it is remembered that the velocity with which light travels is 186,000 miles per second, there should not be any difficulty in supposing that thought-vibrations, or whatever they may be, are propagated through space at an equal or even greater rate of speed. It is not a question, in either case, of any substance being transmitted, or of the absolute simultaneity of emission and reception. And to believe that thoughts may be communicated from soul to soul with the velocity of light does not compel the belief that souls are able to travel from place to place in an equally speedy manner.

CHAPTER IV

DISCARNATE SPIRITS

THE existence of discarnate spirits has been proved in Chapter I. It is desirable now to state what is known as to the conditions in which they exist.

These conditions have been for thousands of years the subject-matter of positive statements. The sacred writings and inscriptions, and the traditions of the various religions that have flourished in olden times or are still professed are full of descriptions of the religions in which discarnate spirits pass their time and of the manner of their lives in the spirit-world. Magicians, wizards, witches and necromancers of all kinds have, it is said, received copious information to the same effect. And during the last seventy years Spiritualistic literature has added abundantly to the common stock.

In spite, however, of all this, great uncertainty prevails. The statements to which reference has been made are, in well-nigh all cases, of what is called an "unverifiable" character; that is to say, they are not capable of test and confirmation by any mundane methods of en-quiry. But although an unverifiable assertion is incapable of normal proof it may still be capable of disproof. If, for example, it be self-contradictory it must, of course, be rejected. And if two separate unverifiable statements contradict each other it is obvious that they cannot both be true: one of them, at least, must be false, while the other remains doubtful. Furthermore, if an unverifiable piece of information be opposed to some clearly-estab-lished fact or well-proved doctrine no reasonable person will regard it as worthy of credence.

This book is not concerned with the question of whether the accounts of miracles and other supernor-mal details in the Bible are or are not to be believed. The purely religious view of the matter need not be dwelt upon. Nor will it be of any practical utility to take into consideration the history of magic and the doings of magicians as distinguished in the popular idea from religion and its ministers. What is alone needful to be mentioned is the evidence that has been more or less sci-entifically accumulated in modern times in connection with psychical phenomena and with communications understood to have taken place across the border-line between living humanity and the spirit-world. Much of this evidence is, as has already been said, unverifi-able, and a good deal of it can be disproved. But there remains a very substantial residuum that demands rec-ognition and acceptance by men of education who are free from prejudice and willing to be guided by reason; and this is the trustworthy source of a certain degree of precise knowledge with regard to the conditions of life beyond death.

The most striking fact that thus comes under observation is the readiness with which communication can be opened up with discarnate spirits by persons who are naturally capable of recognising their presence. It happens frequently that in less than a minute after the commencement of a "sitting" indications are given of one or more spirits being in attendance; and it is very rarely indeed that any sitting remains altogether blank. If, then, we reflect that since "Spiritualism" has become a cult sittings have taken place, and are still taking place, day by day, week in and week out, and from year's end to year's end, we are forced to regard this world as being still the habitat of many a discarnate spirit. The conclusion thus arrived at is confirmed by the less systematic phenomena of dreams, phantoms, haunting, "possession," second-sight, clairvoyance, automatic speech and writing, the spontaneous movements of material objects and other like occurrences; merely, however, to the extent of their being really due to the denizens of the spirit-world, which is acknowledged to be the case in many instances.

The certainty thus arising that great numbers of spirits do not leave the earth when they become separated from the human bodies they have inhabited suggests a doubt as to whether any spirits at all go to some other sphere. The evidence available does not remove the doubt. It is true that discarnate spirits sometimes volunteer statements with regard to another world, and sometimes in reply to questions give particulars as to their residence in such a region. But this information is of the unverifiable kind, is often "nonsense," as Sir Oliver Lodge has said, and is frequently demonstrably false; while it is always discredited by the fact that the spirit who claims to be a resident in a far-distant sphere of being is nevertheless self-admittedly present in a London room or wherever else the sitting may take place. The contradiction is never explained away in any reasonable manner. It may be said, therefore, to be highly probable that death merely opens the way to a further term of existence in this world, and that the spirits of the departed remain for the period of such term in the more or less near neighbourhood of the relatives and friends they have left behind them. The idea of such post-mortem existence being also limited in time arises naturally, and is to be reasonably inferred, from the evidence now being considered. Although discarnate spirits are very numerous, their number, so far as they manifest themselves, is altogether insignificant when compared with that of the deaths that occur from day to day; while if we take into account the consideration that the entire soul-population of the earth becomes discarnate from generation to generation, that is to say, every thirty years or so, we are faced by the fact that living persons are but as a drop in the ocean of possible individual existences. We have also to bear in mind that each of these existences is separate from the rest, and does not originate either from nothing or from inanimate matter or from inanimate energy, as may possibly be the case with Life. If, then, souls when disembodied remain perpetually in this world, it follows, first, that there must be a continual supply of fresh souls coming in from some other region of the universe; and, secondly, that of all these millions of millions of active intelligences only one, here and there, is able or willing to make its presence known to mankind. These conclusions are of so extravagant a character as to be unacceptable; and if it be possible to frame an hypothesis that avoids the difficulties they involve, it would be a reasonable proceeding to adopt such an alternative view.

Psychical philosophy has in all ages been furnished with at least one "working hypothesis" of the kind required. Its scientific name is "metempsychosis," which in more popular language is known as "transmigration." It teaches that after death the spirit enters into some other human body which happens to be living and unprovided with a soul; and the doctrine is frequently extended to include the idea that the new habitat may even be the body of one of the lower animals. Many of the most famous thinkers of Greece and the Orient were associated with the belief in question. It is to be found in the Bible and other sacred writings, and forms a part of the religions of many races throughout the world. It cannot, therefore, be lightly disregarded as a mere fantasy unworthy of consideration by civilised people in the twentieth century.

As a matter of fact, the theory of transmigration fits in with modern observations. It does away with the necessity of a perpetual supply of fresh souls from extra-mundane regions. It also is consistent with, and explains, the absence of any vast overwhelming spirit-population. Moreover, it is the logical concomitant of our common, everyday experience. We are familiar with the occurrence of what we call "births," that is, the coming into existence of new human bodies. We know also that these new bodies become, in some way or other, the temporary abodes of souls—the tenancy being sometimes a matter of minutes only and sometimes enduring for rather more than one hundred years. We see for ourselves that the habitation suits the tenant and that the tenant suits the habitation. What, then, can be more natural and fitting than that, when the tenant, for some reason or another, has to quit his dwelling, he looks out for another abode of much the same kind? So far from this course of action being fantastic and improbable, it is pre-eminently likely. The play of mere imagination is to be found altogether with those mental speculators who talk of the supposed departure of discarnate spirits to supposed spheres of existence beyond the earth.

It is quite conceivable, and probable enough, that some little time elapses between "death" and "reincarnation." Hence it is to be expected that there is always a greater or less number of discarnate spirits dwelling temporarily, and a little disconsolately, perhaps, in the air-occupied space surrounding the earth; and this expectation is borne out by actual observation. It is to be surmised, furthermore, that spirits awaiting re-embodiment will feel themselves more at home, as it were, if they remain in the immediate proximity of the localities they inhabited and the persons they knew before "death." Here, again, we find the surmise to accord with experience. Some places are undoubtedly "haunted"; and it is equally certain that some persons are haunted also; for it would otherwise be impossible to account reasonably for the well-known fact that sitters at séances habitually open up communications with their deceased relatives and friends who have always been perfect strangers to the mediums with whom the sittings take place. The spirits are not brought by the mediums; they are introduced by the sitters themselves, who are quite unconscious of being thus accompanied or "haunted" To deny this is equivalent to maintaining the absurdity that every real medium is en rapport with all the deceased relatives and friends of every living human being. The soul of a medium is not endowed with powers vastly greater than those of ordinary souls; any more than a discarnate spirit is able to know and do very much beyond what he was aware of or could accomplish during life. If either mediums or spirits were capable of really marvellous achievements we may be sure that now and again some daring soul would contrive to startle mankind; and as no such feat has been recorded through the ages ("miracles" religious and otherwise, are not here referred to), it is a fair inference that our deceased friends are not vastly different from, or, at any rate, are not vastly superior to, what they were when we knew them here.

Coming now to the question of the form in which discarnate spirits exist, all the available evidence of a verifiable or logically-acceptable character goes to show that in the spirit-world there are not any differences of type corresponding to what are found among human beings. Spirits are not white, black, brown, yellow and red; they are not Anglo-Saxon, Teutonic, Scandinavian, Gaelic, Arab, negro, Mongolian or Polynesian. If the contrary were the case it would, by this time, have become apparent. Something of this lack of evidence may perhaps be due to the fact that modern psychical research has for the most part been conducted by English and American investigators, while most of the communications with spirits have involved the use of the English language and have been recorded in that tongue. Hence it is to be supposed that the spirits who have taken part in the proceedings have been only those possessing a knowledge of English; yet, even in that case, souls of many earthly races might have been expected to come forward. And as the same argument applies to the less numerous instances of psychical investigations by French, Italian, Spanish, German, Swedish, Russian, etc, students of the occult, the conclusion is inevitable that spirits are not divided into racial categories even though they may differ in what may be termed bodily characteristics and developments.

That spirits have organised bodies is clear. The "stuff" of which their bodies are made is, however, not ordinary matter. We already know by Dr. Crawford's experiments—mentioned in Chapter I of this book—that a something exists which gravitates and yet is invisible to our eyes. We also know, by common psychical experience, that spirits are able to see, hear, speak and touch, and can by us be seen, heard, spoken to and touched. If these facts be co-ordinated they do not leave any room for doubt as to there being spiritual equivalents of human bodies equipped with organs of sense and perception. It does not follow necessarily that these equivalents are counterparts or facsimiles in form and appearance, even if in many of their functions they are practically indistinguishable from their human prototypes. Racial peculiarities are admittedly absent, as also is Life with its physiological requirements. Spirits are free from wear and tear, from the need of food, clothing and shelter, and from the maintenance of health. They are not divided by sex differences and they are not characterised by any form of reproduction: they have neither ancestry nor posterity. These various features lend force to the theory of transmigration. They show the possibility of an ordinary human body being permeated, so to say, by a spirit's body which can enter or leave at any time and which always maintains its separate existence. Here, again, there are facts of common knowledge and experience that support the doctrine of metempsychosis.

Most persons are, now and then, conscious of memories or reminiscent impressions that cannot be traced to any events of the present life. It occasionally happens that when a person first visits some particular locality he finds himself in surroundings with which his mind is already familiar. The only reasonable explanation is that the soul remembers somewhat of its experiences in a previous earthly life.

Another line of thought leading in the same direction is that suggested by the marked and well-known phenomena of mental heredity. Family peculiarities of mind and character are commonly supposed to be transmitted from parents to children in the form of material germs which are imagined, but have never been proved, to exist. And yet in many cases—as also happens with physical peculiarities—an intervening generation is skipped, and it is the mental characteristic of a grandparent or great-grandparent that reappears in the descendant. It would, therefore, seem more reasonable to infer that the true cause of heredity is to be found in the preference manifested by discarnate spirits for reincarnation in the direct posterity of the human bodies they have at one time or another inhabited. Nor is it a far-fetched supposition to hold that, in the spirit-world, as in this life, souls of similar characters associate together and, to whatever extent may be possible, seek to be reincarnated in the same earthly families: a supposition that accounts for more than one child of a family presenting what are considered to be the hereditary characteristics. It should not, however, be concluded that soul and body are without reaction on each other. We know, as a fact, that mental habits and emotional indulgences gradually affect a person's features and disturb the functioning of various organs. We also know that bodily peculiarities warp the mind and influence the thoughts. The phrenological mapping of the brain has some foundation in reality; and probably there does not exist a single person of mature age who is not to some extent a physiognomist. Intelligent capacity, sensitiveness and moral character do, most undoubtedly, depend a good deal upon the size, form and texture of the brain. In other words, a soul when in the body is fettered and guided and is not fully able to reveal its true self. From this it follows that when a soul becomes separated from the body it cannot logically be expected to have exactly the same character that it apparently possessed in life. Psychical experience in spiritualistic sittings and otherwise is to this effect. It is customary, indeed, for sitters to say—and, emotionally, to believe—that the spirits of their deceased relatives and friends behave and speak exactly as they used to do in life; but this is not quite borne out by the recorded evidence. It is customary also, where the discrepancies are of too glaring a nature to be glozed over or hushed up, to put them down to the interference of mischievous spirits who personate the spirits called for; but this is a very lame method of explanation. The best plan in all cases of difficulty is to face boldly the facts. A disembodied spirit is less cribbed, cabined and confined than when it was attached to a living body; it is more free for both good and evil. We are familiar enough with good, bad and indifferent souls in this world: why should we expect the same souls to be otherwise simply because of a change in their environment? All that we can reasonably look for is a certain degree of revelation, a certain manifestation of what before was more or less hidden and which may be estimable or the reverse.

A feature that deserves notice as related to this view of the matter is the consensus of testimony to the effect that communicating spirits, whether those who are sought for or those who are what may be termed casual and errant, have habitually a less regard for truth than is the case with highly-educated human beings; though, if an average be struck of mankind in general, it does not seem that there is much to choose between the trustworthiness of statements made by the living inhabitants of the earth and the truth of what is said by disembodied spirits. Still, the matter is of some importance, seeing that it bears very materially upon the question of whether individual spirits are always the particular disembodied souls they profess to be.

Another feature, equally worthy of attention, is the apparent absence of spirits who can properly be regarded as diabolical. Sittings for the purpose of communication with "surviving" souls are not attended by devils or by beings occupied mainly in the pursuit of evil. It may, of course, be the case that the published records and the verbal accounts that are current suppress all mention of occurrences deemed to be demoniacal, in the same way that, according to Sir Oliver Lodge, spiritualists "usually either discourage or suppress" statements "about the nature of things 'on the other side.'" The eminent authority here quoted goes on, indeed, to say—

"These are what we call the 'unverifiable' communications; for we cannot bring them to book by subsequent terrestrial inquiry in the same way as we can test information concerning personal or mundane affairs. Information of the higher kind has often been received but has seldom been published; and it is difficult to know what value to put upon it, or how far it is really trustworthy."

This very frank confession of the reports of séances being systematically garbled is a little disconcerting, especially when coming from one of the shining lights of the scientific world; but it probably means no more than that the champions of spiritualism do not desire to arouse antagonism that can be avoided. In the same way it may well be that those persons who, whether as mediums or sitters or in the privacy of individual attempts at communication, happen to come into contact with evil spirits do not feel disposed to subject themselves to the hostility of the religious world by detailing their experiences. But, however this may be, the fact remains that, so far as common knowledge and common repute are concerned, the devilish element is not likely to be encountered by those persons who seek to speak with the dead.

If, now, the particulars set forth in the present chapter be summarised we find the state of things to be as follows:—

1. Disembodied souls do not depart from this world when "death" occurs.
2. They remain for a time free from bodily environment of an ordinary material kind.
3. Sooner or later they enter into new human bodies, and perhaps, also, in some cases, into new bodies of the lower animals.
4. During the period of their free existence while awaiting transmigration, many of them make a practice of haunting localities and living human beings.
5. They possess in themselves the equivalent of bodies constructed of something analogous to matter

and having organisms by which they perceive and act.

6. Each disembodied soul is an individual entity existing permanently apart from all others and not distinguished by any racial or sexual characteristics.

7. Each individual soul has its own idiosyncrasies of intellect, sense, emotion, conscience and volition. These idiosyncrasies are subject to at least temporary modification by the association of the soul with a human body.

8. The character and conduct of a disembodied soul are not necessarily the same in all respects as were apparent during life, and do not necessarily remain completely unchanged when transmigration takes place.

9. The existence of souls that are wholly evil has not yet been established by actual observation or experience of any kind.

This summary does not involve any religious views and is not based on any religious teaching. It is essentially scientific; that is to say, it puts into plain language the conclusions arrived at by impartial students of physical and psychical facts and phenomena, irrespective of whether such conclusions do or do not fit in with ecclesiastical teaching, popular notions, or "sceptical" dogmatism.

At the same time it is to be observed that the view here taken of discarnate spirits leaves the ground quite open for Religion. It is quite consistent with the existence of a Divine Ruler, with the doctrine of progression in either rightdoing or wrongdoing, and with an Eternal

Justice that inflicts punishment upon souls whose volition is employed for base purposes. For example, it may
well be that in transmigration the choice does not always
rest with the soul concerned, but is divinely decreed; the
new life may be higher or lower than the preceding life,
according to whether the latter was turned to good or
bad account. The number of transmigrations of any
particular soul may be limited; and metempsychosis
may thus correspond to the doctrine of Purgatory—an
evolutionary period at the conclusion of which the soul
is transferred to a Heaven or Hell beyond the confines
of the earth. Even the idea of a Holy Ghost that contin-
ually appeals to the mind and will is not excluded from
the psychical summary above given; nor is there therein anything that contradicts the theory of a Christ or a
Buddha. What the truth is with regard to such matters
as these must be determined by each person for himself
or herself. The readers of the present volume are not
addressed as Christians or as non-Christians, as Deists
or as Atheists. They are considered merely as being interested in the subject of speaking with the dead, and as
being desirous of receiving information with regard to
the ascertained facts and admitted logic of the matter.

CHAPTER V

MEDIUMS

INEQUALITY is the rule of the universe. It is particularly observable in the characters and capacities of human beings. Many persons are musicians; others are incapable of playing the simplest musical instrument. A few individuals, here and there, are mathematicians; the great majority of mankind are not even good arithmeticians. Artists exist in considerable numbers; but they are sparse compared with the duller souls. Chess-players are rarities. Really good, unselfish, high-principled souls, steadfast in the practice of righteousness and unswayed by prejudice, convention and dogma, are seldom met with.

It is not to be wondered at, therefore, that the possession of minds and brains capable of being affected by external psychical influences is not found to be a common characteristic of people in general. In past ages, magicians, seers, wizards, witches and the like, have been the exception, not the rule; and in modern times, when these singularly-constituted beings are called "mediums," their numbers still remain very restricted. That real mediums do, in point of fact, exist to some extent is certain. Thus, Sir Oliver Lodge says, in "Raymond"—

"Do we understand how a mind [= soul] can with difficulty and imperfectly operate another body submitted to its temporary guidance and control? No. Do we know for a fact that it does? Aye, that is the question—a question of evidence. I myself answer the question affirmatively; not on theoretical grounds—far from that—but on a basis of straightforward experience. Others, if they allow themselves to take the trouble to get the experience, will come to the same conclusions. . . . Let us be as cautious and critical, aye, and as sceptical as we like, but let us also be patient and persevering and fair; do not let us start with a preconceived notion of what is possible and what is impossible in this almost unexplored universe; let us only be willing to learn and be guided by facts, and not dogmas: and gradually the truth will permeate our understanding and make for itself a place in our minds as secure as in any other branch of observational science."

He says, moreover, when alluding to speaking with the dead—

Communication is not easy, but it occurs; and humanity has reason to be grateful to those few individuals who, finding themselves possessed of the faculty of mediumship, and therefore able to act as intermediaries, allow themselves to be used for this purpose."

The nature of the peculiarities—anatomical, physiological or psychical, or perhaps all three combined—that distinguish a medium from other human beings is not yet known, and no means of inspection as yet exist by which to be certain that any particular person is or is not a medium. Actual experience is the only guide. This, of course, leaves the door open to the fraudulent assumption of mediumship. But the occurrence of fraud and imposture does not affect the existence of genuine mediums. In every profession are to be found similar examples of deceit. Have not all educated persons heard of "pious frauds" perpetrated by the holders of high religious office? Are there not many instances of ignorant, venal and deliberately unjust judges? Do statesmen and politicians always reject bribes and act solely for the good of their countries? Does a physician invariably admit his inability to understand a complaint; and do general practitioners in every case administer real medicines instead of the proverbial "bread pills" and "coloured water"? Do manufacturers and traders deal solely in unadulterated goods? When these questions can be satisfactorily answered it will be time enough to put the entire profession of mediums in the pillory; and until then all reasonable men and women will be content to recognise that in mediumship, as in other pursuits, we must expect to meet with both the worthy and the unworthy.

What, perhaps, is not yet fully recognised is that mediums are much more numerous than would appear to be the case if regard be had solely to the professional class, that is, to the persons who practise mediumship as a means of livelihood. There are many amateur "mediums"; and there are also many other individuals who are conscious of possessing what are spoken of as "psychic powers," and yet either do not allow the fact to become known or confine the exercise of their powers to the de-

velopment of communications in their own private surroundings. Hence, if every professional medium without
exception were shown to be a fraud—which is not the
case now, and never has been the case at any time—
there would still remain an abundance of trustworthy
experiential and experimental evidence establishing the
reality of speaking with the dead. For instance, the Mrs.
Kennedy who plays such an important part in the story
of "Raymond" is not a professional medium at all; she
is the wife of a London physician, leads the life of an ordinary private English lady moving in good society, and
is not paid for any aid she may render to friends who
are desirous of "communicating." So, too, the medium,
Miss Goligher, who assists Dr. Crawford is a young lady
of private social position, who gives her services with the
approval and aid of her family and without fee or re-
ward, except, of course, such moral satisfaction as may
arise from the consciousness of being engaged in a work
likely to benefit mankind.

It often happens that mediums are ignorant and il-
literate; and there is not any case on record where a medium, whether educated or uneducated, has been able to
give an intelligible account of the way in which communications with disembodied souls become possible. As a
general rule real mediums do not claim a greater knowledge of psychical phenomena than is possessed by the
sitters themselves. They are aware that communications
take place, and they find by actual experience that they
themselves serve as intermediaries. Beyond this they do
not seek to enquire; and they refrain from attempting
in any way to control the proceedings. They are passive instruments in the hands of the powers from "the
other side"; much as was the case, we read, with those

persons who gave voice to the oracles of old. In view of these facts it seems to follow that the common practice of "testing" the mediums and putting constraint upon them is a mere waste of time and attention. If they be genuine they are, virtually, mere pieces of mechanism; and all that can be done usefully is to observe the working. If they be fraudulent this will quickly enough become self-evident. All that the sitter need do is to bring a little common sense to bear.

It is a vexed question whether professional mediums are or are not banded together in a secret craft or guild for the purpose of collecting and interchanging information with regard to sitters and their families. The suggestion of such a combination apparently implies a doubt as to the good faith of mediums in general; but another interpretation is possible. It must be remembered that old laws are still in existence which forbid any exploitation of asserted psychical powers. These laws have produced a long series of "common informers," who under various pretences arrange sittings with mediums for the purpose of entrapping them into breaches of the law, irrespective of whether the phenomena observed are or are not genuine. It would therefore be a very natural proceeding for mediums to co-operate for the object of self-protection. But as regards any attempts to "arrange" the communications the futility of such proceedings is obvious. Sitters turn up unexpectedly from all localities. They may or they may not give their right names and addresses. Where the séance takes place at once there is not any opportunity of instituting any enquiry. And it is perfectly clear that a medium in any particular locality cannot keep in stock a mass of information with regard to private individuals in the rest of the country. The

"sceptic," or critic, therefore, who indulges in the belief that communications can be explained away by the
theory that all mediums are dishonest, and have been at
every sitting in previous possession of the information
conveyed in the alleged utterances of the spirits, is very
much more credulous than the most gullible sitter.

Although it is correct to regard the medium as a
mechanism by means of which the spirits are able to
communicate with living persons, it would be a mistake
to overlook the fact that the mechanism possesses an individuality which to some extent qualifies the communications. Every man knows that his handwriting varies
with every change of pen. Delicate embroidery is not
practicable with darning-needles. A discarnate soul that
finds itself compelled to use a medium's hand for writing
or a medium's vocal apparatus for speaking has to actu-
ate these organs by means of the medium's brain, which
may be, so to speak, either coarse or fine, and in every
case is attuned by the experiences of its normal life. The
medium's habits of thought and expression thus become
intermingled with and sometimes quite override those
of the communicating spirit; and this "sophistication,"
as it is termed, leads frequently to much confusion and
many errors of statement. It also serves to accentuate in
appearance the change of character, already mentioned
in these pages, that is often observed in disembodied
spirits when compared with their demeanour during
life. Great care is necessary, therefore, in judging how
far communications through mediums are to be taken
at their face values. It is not a question of good or bad
faith. The point involved is whether any, and what, al-
lowance should be made for the imperfection of the instruments employed.

Many mediums—the great majority, in fact—assert, and are genuinely convinced, that they work under the control of certain individual spirits. This has always been claimed in magical circles; and a good deal of evidence exists to support a belief in the reality of "familiar spirits." At the same time it is difficult for unprejudiced observers to accept the idea of there being any spirits who are content to dance attendance day and night and year after year upon human beings of a very ordinary type and undistinguished by any great qualities of soul. This difficulty is increased when consideration is given to what is said with respect to the "controls" themselves. They adopt names that are fantastic and arbitrarily assumed; they never give any confirmable information as to their identities and abodes when in life; their professed individualities—little Indian girls, Indian yogis, Indian chiefs, unknown "doctors," etc.—are constantly in palpable contradiction with their own utterances and doings; and they remain in evidence only so long as their respective mediums continue in professional work. The theory is sometimes advanced that a "control" is a "second personality" of the medium—a supposition that meets the difficulties to which allusion has been made. But a "second personality" is, in effect, a second soul, no matter what attempts may be made to whittle down its meaning by talk of "sub-consciousness," "subliminal individuality" and the like. A person who has a second soul is a person who is "possessed" by a spirit entering into the body from the outside and sharing the habitat with its original tenant. It is not necessary to infer that the brain and other bodily organs are used simultaneously by the two souls: the trend of the available evidence is, on the contrary, to show that the normal soul is commonly in sole control and that it is only occasionally that the supernormal occupant takes the reins. But the theory in question does undoubtedly compel a modification of the view usually entertained with regard to mediums. Not only must they all be looked upon as human beings of exceptional physical and psychical characteristics, but in the majority of cases they must be classed in the category of persons who are "possessed." Fortunately the "controls" are rarely, if ever, of a completely evil nature; but there is reason to think that they are occasionally of a type lower than souls in general. Idiocy and insanity are not always accompanied by any clearly-defined disease or malformation of the brain, and in such cases may possibly result from what may be termed the clumsy intermeddling of two distinct soul—both being of an inferior order—in the same bodily environment.

The subject here discussed is not a light and negligible matter where speaking with the dead is concerned. Very many persons find it both convenient and desirable to employ mediums as intermediaries, and in almost every instance this means the additional intervention of some "control." Here, again, it will be useful to make a quotation from "Raymond," the most satisfactory work yet published on "survival" and "communication," and a well-filled store-house of fact and reasoning.

"But however much," says Sir Oliver Lodge, "can be and has been written on this subject, and whatever different opinions may be held, it is universally admitted that the dramatic semblance of the control is undoubtedly that of a separate person [i.e. a soul distinct from the normal soul of the medium]—a person asserted to be permanently existing on the other side and to be occupied on that side in much the same functions as the medium is on this. The duty of controlling and transmitting messages seems to be laid upon such a one— it is his special work. The dramatic character of most of the controls is so vivid and self-consistent, that whatever any given sitter or experimenter may feel is the probable truth concerning their real nature, the simplest way is to humour them by taking them at their face value and treating them as separate and responsible and real individuals. It is true that in the case of some mediums, especially when overdone or tired, there are evanescent and absurd intrusions every now and then, which cannot be seriously regarded. Those have to be eliminated; and for anyone to treat them as real people would be ludicrous; but undoubtedly the serious controls show a character and personality and memory of their own, and they appear to carry on as continuous an existence as anyone else whom one only meets occasionally for a conversation."

There is not anything in this weighty expression of opinion that really clashes with the "possession" theory, except, indeed, the suggestion that the controls are persons "permanently existing on the other side"—a suggestion which is in obvious conflict with the admission that controls are in constant attendance on mediums in this world. What Sir Oliver means by "evanescent and absurd intrusions" that "cannot be seriously regarded" or treated as "real people" is also not clear, but probably refers to some form of "sophistication" resulting from a derangement of the transmitting mechanism. In any case the conclusion remains that the transmission takes place through a combination of medium-cum-control; and this may in great measure explain the apparent psychical sensitiveness of mediums. That is to say, the reason why mediums are particularly subject to spiritual influence from the outside may be due to the fact of their possessing, or being possessed by, a secondary semi-attached soul which is comparatively free to perceive and attend to the efforts made by external spirits to open up communication.

CHAPTER VI

COMMUNICATING

VERY many methods have been discovered of communicating with discarnate spirits; but it is not needful in the present volume to deal with any system of incantation or "magical" rites. What is proposed is to describe such practices as have in modern times been found to yield good results and have become customary.

1. EXPECTANCY

This is suitable where an individual person desires to ascertain whether he or she is endowed with any psychic powers. By sitting in some place quite alone and free from interruption, and by adopting a mental attitude of passive receptivity and expectancy, the soul becomes ready to perceive and be affected by any spirits that may be in its vicinity and that may attempt to open up communications. A Quakers' meeting—though not a case of solitary individuals—is a good illustration of the method of expectancy in actual practice. No one is supposed to speak without being "moved thereto by the Spirit"; and it is by no means an uncommon event for the meeting to begin, continue and end without a single word being said—the necessary vocal impulse being wanting, although various members of the congregation may be distinctly conscious, in a less definite way, of spiritual presence and thought-suggestion.

The manifestations in the course of expectancy sittings may vary from thought-suggestion to positive physical phenomena, such as the sensation of being touched or gently blown upon, the movement of some inanimate object, the hearing of a voice or even the visual appearance of some supernormal object. All depends upon whether the sitter is or is not susceptible to psychical influence, and also upon whether the locality or the sitter personally is or is not haunted. This word "haunted" must not be understood as implying that the sitter—any more than the locality — is conscious of the proximity of spirits or is in any way inconvenienced thereby. It merely means that, as explained in a previous part of this book, discarnate spirits tend to remain near the places and persons with whom they were familiar during life—perhaps in the hope of being able to make their presence known.

2. Automatic Writing

It is very rarely that the results of "expectancy" go beyond thought-impression and subsidiary physical manifestations, neither of which can be regarded as in the nature of practical communications. For the giving of a message or the carrying-on of a conversation something more is required. Accordingly, when an enquirer sits alone it is customary to have at hand a pencil and paper or some apparatus—as, for example, a planchette—by means of which writing is possible. It is then frequently found that the sitter's hand, without any conscious guidance by the sitter, will manipulate the pencil or the apparatus so as to produce a "script" on the paper. This is read and may be followed up by viva voce comments and questions, and thus a regular verbal interview takes place. Automatic writing does not depend upon solitude. It may take place in the presence of any number of observers, and is frequently employed by mediums as being an expeditious method of communication.

3. Trance Writing and Speaking

In cases where the sitter is markedly "psychic" and adopts the method of Expectancy it frequently happens that normal control over the body is lost. A condition of trance supervenes, and while this continues the spirit—which may be either a "second personality" or a soul from the outside—that has gained the upper hand makes use to a greater or less extent of the brain and other organs subject to its mastery. The hand may write: the mouth may speak: the whole body may be engaged in some impersonation; and all this may take place beyond the scope of the sitter's normal consciousness. When the trance is over the sitter is not able to recall anything that has been written or said or enacted. The services of some recording observer are therefore necessary if any practical result is to be obtained.

The trance condition is particularly likely to occur when the sitter, or one of the sitters, is a genuine "medium," or, in other words, a person who either is naturally endowed with special susceptibility to psychical influences or is the habitat of two souls, normal and "subliminal" respectively. Accordingly in the majority of séances with professional mediums the communications from discarnate spirits are received during trance, and take the form of script executed by the medium's hand or words spoken by the medium. Frequently, moreover, the medium is not completely entranced but retains partial consciousness; the result being that what may be described as a dazed condition ensues, and the utterances from "the other side" become mixed with, and qualified by, various halting and imperfect statements emanating from the medium's own mind. This is why so many of the published reports of spiritualistic séances contain what appear to be merely such erroneous and ignorant remarks as might be expected from comparatively uneducated persons who have become acquainted with the tricks of a trade. And as the simulation of a partially-entranced and semi-conscious state is a very easy matter for persons who have any dramatic turn, it is often difficult to know how far a communication is genuine and how far it is inadvertently or designedly sophisticated. But if the recipients of the communication do not allow themselves to be swayed by emotion, and bring a little common sense to bear, they will find in the great majority of cases that the matter can be made clear enough for all practical purposes.

4. Signalling

Communication need not be confined to writing and speech. It is found that codes of signals can be arranged with discarnate spirits desirous of opening up intelligent relations with living persons.

The methods of signalling depend upon the ingenuity and preferences of the parties concerned. They are not restricted to any particular proceedings; though it has become customary with the majority of sitters to make use of "raps" and "table-tilting." It is also usual to agree with the spirits that a single rap or tilting movement shall signify "No," that three raps or tilts shall mean "Yes," and that words shall be conveyed letter by letter, the system adopted being for the living person to pronounce the letters of the alphabet in their due order and for the spirit to give a rap or tilt when the right letter is reached.

It must not, however, be supposed that the employment of a table is in any way necessary. The method has come into vogue merely because people assembling together for intercourse with discarnate spirits have found it convenient to sit round a table. Any idea that spirits have a predilection for, or an attachment to, a table or any other article of furniture is a popular delusion and is most assuredly contrary to common sense. All available evidence goes to show that spirits find much greater difficulty in operating on matter than on mind. The setting of any physical mass in motion is a particularly arduous task; and the work becomes lighter in proportion as the mass to be moved is smaller and less weighty. To expect a spirit to set a bulky article like a table in movement is unreasonable; and the fact that tables are moved by spirits is not an argument to the contrary. Spirits are sometimes asked how they contrive to do such physical work, and a conventional reply has become current, namely, that the sitters "supply magnetism which is gathered in the medium and goes into the table." From a scientific point of view this answer is nonsensical. It is, in all probability, a "sophistication" repeated, wittingly or unwittingly, by medium after medium. Another explanation which is put forward occasionally seems to be nearer the mark, i.e. that where heavy articles are moved the work is done by a number of spirits acting together.

However all this may be, it is clear that those sitters who use less cumbrous means than tables for signalling are more likely to be satisfied. And it is also clear that the customary "once for No" and "three times for Yes" are not imperative. Any other code may be adopted. Communications are not subject to any arbitrary regulations. They have all the freedom of ordinary personal intercourse.

5. DIRECT MESSAGES

These have already been mentioned under the heading of Expectancy; but they are occasionally found to occur in conjunction with other methods of communicating. A pencil is sometimes seen to be apparently writing of its own accord on a sheet of paper; no human hand being near it. Sometimes it is seen to be guided by the simulacrum of a hand—a phenomenon that takes place more frequently when the sitting is held in a dimly-lighted locality or even in the dark. In the latter case the visibility is due to the object seen being self-luminous. The script produced by such direct writing is, of course, the message to be received.

In like manner a message is sometimes conveyed by a voice which is unconnected with any person present at the sitting; and the utterance may vary from a whisper addressed to some individual ear to a loud discourse audible by the whole company.

6. MATERIALISATION

This is a development of direct communication. The spirit becomes either visible or tangible, and sometimes is both. Its form and appearance are akin to those of a clothed human being; though the similarity is not in any way complete. The substance of which such phantasms are composed is as yet unknown to science; but its perceptibility by normal sight and touch suggests a material character, without, however, necessitating the idea of solidity any more than in the case of an evanescent cloud or mist. So, too, the form assumed must not be regarded as being necessarily the real form of the spirit in the apparition, the tenuous substance of which is obviously capable of any desired configuration; while the comparative rarity of the phenomenon implies that it is only here and there that a spirit is found possessing the requisite knowledge and artistic capacity for the work of putting together and shaping such a production.

Some of the materialised beings seem unable to speak or to display much power of movement. Others can speak and move about with facility. Others again can handle various objects, such as musical instruments, books, flowers and the like, and can convey them from place to place.

The manifestations here touched upon are much more frequent in dark séances than in the light; and even when some degree of illumination is allowed the usual practice is to provide "cabinets" or screens under the cover of which the psychical effects are developed. This naturally gives ample opportunity for trickery to persons who, whether for money-making or for other motives, pose as mediums without having any real qualifications for the work; and it is unquestionable that many instances of sham materialisations have from time to time taken place. On the other hand, the well-evidenced instances of real materialisations and of many other analogous kinds of psycho-physical phenomena are much more numerous. We must consider, moreover, that a good reason exists for dim light and darkness in connection with attempts to communicate with discarnate spirits. When the eyes are active the mind receives continual impressions of numerous objects and occurrences that engage its attention and render it much less receptive of occult influences. Hence by minimising or shutting out the distractions of sight the soul of a sitter becomes very much more attuned to whatever telepathy may exist in connection with such external spirits as are present.

With regard to communicating in general the old proverb, "Practice makes perfect," holds good. Mediums, it is true, are born, not made; but, as is the case with all human beings, their powers are at first immature, and have to be developed by long-continued exercise and more or less skilled training before the best results become attainable. Every person who wishes to speak with the dead is—as is also every other person in the world—at least a potential medium so far as he or she knows at the outset. If it be found on trial that psychic powers exist to an appreciable extent it may be taken for granted that they are capable of very great increase by persevering effort and systematic employment; and the growth may be such as to lead through the lower to the higher forms of communicating. If, however, after repeated experiments it appears that a susceptibility to psychical influences is lacking or very moderate in degree, or if, for any other reason, a continuance of personal effort be not desirable, then it becomes necessary to have recourse to the services of mediums. These latter may be either amateur or professional; but, whichever they are, their utility depends upon the stage of development they have reached.

The term "development" as here used means an increased sensitiveness of the perceptive faculty by which the medium becomes aware of and influenced by the proximity of discarnate spirits. It means also an intensified passivity of the normal soul, thus facilitating control by the secondary mind or by external spirits. And it signifies furthermore the placing of a larger proportion of the medium's substance and physical powers at the disposal of the controlling beings, thereby enabling these existences to produce manifestations which otherwise would be impossible. The actual modus operandi of the use by a control of a medium's body and vitality is not yet understood; but the fact of such use has been a matter of observation and experiment in all ages of which we have any record. Hence the communication with a discarnate spirit will be fuller, freer and more extended in proportion to the better adaptation of the intermediate psychical mechanism.

CHAPTER VII

PRACTICAL INSTRUCTIONS FOR
SPEAKING WITH THE DEAD

1.—As a general rule applying to all methods of communicating, every person who desires to be brought into touch with discarnate spirits should make a point of being tranquil, unoccupied, serious and attentive. There are two reasons for this. First, it is obvious that a mind free from outside cares and distractions is able to concentrate itself in any desired direction, and can become aware of influences that would pass unnoticed in the ordinary hurly-burly of life. Secondly, a soul at rest can be impressed by other souls very much more readily than when it is busy with activities of its own.

2.—The best method to adopt at the outset is that of Expectancy (see Chapter VI). The enquirer should sit quite alone in some room free from interruption—an indoors sitting, by reason of its fewer distractions, being preferable to a sitting in any out-of-doors locality.

The thoughts need not take any religious turn, and prayer is quite unnecessary. It is desirable, in fact, to think as little as possible about anything, except in the event of the presence of some particular spirit being hoped for. When that is the case the mind may with advantage be occupied by reminiscences connected with the spirit in question—a situation being thus created which much facilitates telepathy and is analogous to the hoisting of a signal calling for response.

The evening is the most suitable time for an Expectancy sitting, which is to be held in the light or in semi-obscurity; the bustle and turmoil of the day having then given place more or less to quietude and tranquillity. But, if darkness does not inspire fear, a sitting in a bedroom (or other apartment) during the hours from midnight to, say, two o'clock in the morning is preferable. Silence is then more supreme than at any other time, and the majority of the human beings in the locality are asleep. This accounts for the traditional notion of "the witching hour," which is not based, as is supposed erroneously, on some divine or diabolical limitation of certain hours as the free time for errant spirits. It refers to the fact that sleep is a kind of trance during which the hold of the body on the soul is slackened, thus facilitating the task of any outside spirit who may wish to communicate; the point in issue being well exemplified by the old Romans (and others of the ancients), who taught that dreams are the apparitions of supernormal beings. Dealing first with the case of a midnight sitting, it should be noted that absolute darkness is not imperative. The room may be illuminated in any way that is convenient; but, for reasons already given, the less light the better. If the nerves of the sitter will bear the strain the sitting should take place quite in the dark. In that event some apparatus for signalling by sound should be provided, such as, for instance, a small key suspended by a thread inside a glass tumbler in such a manner that a very slight movement is accompanied by a tinkling.

After remaining quiet and expectant for a few minutes the sitter should speak aloud and ask, "Are there any spirits present?" This requires a little courage, both physical and moral; the former because of the darkness, the "witching hour" and the sound of one's voice in the stillness; and the latter because one is tempted to regard both the situation and the question as absurd, and because one does not relish the idea of possibly making a fool of one's self. But it is merely a question of breaking the ice. When once the sitter has spoken aloud the difficulty of speaking does not recur.

To ask in one's mind whether there are any spirits present is not as effective as actual speech. There is a greater psychical concentration when a) thought is focussed, as it were, by spoken words; besides which there is some reason to believe that spirits—the bodily substance and organs of whom are analogous to those of living persons—find it easier to receive impressions by physical sounds than by telepathy.

If no answer be given to the question, this should be repeated with a request that the spirit or spirits will reply by causing the suspended key to move in such a manner as to produce three distinct tinklings—or words to the same general effect in the case of some other signalling apparatus being employed. If there still be silence, it may be concluded either that no spirit is present in the room on that particular occasion, or that no spirit within hearing understands the English language, or that the prevailing temporary conditions do not allow of physical effects being produced on inanimate matter, or that the sitter, by lack of psychic power, is unable to attract the attention of discarnate spirits.

If a reply be given, it is not a matter of course for it to take the form requested. Instead of being a tinkling or other specified signal, it may be a rustling, a rap, a tapping, a scratching, a pattering, a sigh, a movement of the air or of some object in the room, a sensation of cold, a sound as of whispering, a faint luminosity, a touch, etc. Hence the necessity for the sitter to be keenly on the alert and completely attentive, while at the same time remaining perfectly tranquil and collected; for some indication of a spirit being present may be given by the latter spontaneously before any word is spoken.

When once any sign of communication is observed the sitter should announce the fact and should ask for it to be repeated, and if this be done a signalling code may thereupon be adopted by agreement and a conversation may take place accordingly. If, on the other hand, there be no sign at all during the period of, say, half an hour from the commencement of the sitting, this latter should terminate and the enquirer should renew the attempt on some future occasion. No disappointment need be felt at a negative result, whether at the outset of the experiments or at any particular sitting. Conditions are not always favourable, even with the same sitter and in the same room; and in spite of widely-prevalent ideas and the records of spiritualistic séances, it is quite idle to suppose that) disembodied souls do, in fact, cater for the arbitrary wishes and personal convenience of human beings. Nothing of the kind can be taken for granted, except, indeed, that matter-void space has its inhabitants just as much as is the case with any matter-occupied locality, and that any room in any house is just as likely to be visited from time to time by discarnate spirits as by living persons.

Coming now to what may be termed ordinary Expectancy sittings, that is to say, evening sittings in a lighted or semi-lighted room, the conditions of visibility admit of more elaborate manifestations than are possible in darkness. Automatic writing in particular becomes practicable. Provision should be made for this by placing a pencil and one or more sheets of paper on a table or desk. And, of course, signalling apparatus should be furnished of either an audible or a visible kind. When these matters are attended to the proceedings at the sitting should follow the course described as suitable for the midnight séance; but, naturally, both eyes and ears should be active in the detection of signs indicating the presence of spirits. And every now and then the pencil should be taken in the hand and held close to the paper in a writing position, the result frequently being that a strong impulse to write is felt. This should not be resisted. The hand should be given free play; but, of course, there should not be any conscious guidance by the sitter. At first the script is, in the majority of instances, found to be a confused scribble or a meaningless sequence of words. Later on, if the sitter be patient and persevering, order begins to take the place of chaos and intelligible messages are obtained; always supposing that the enquirer is really gifted with an appreciable degree of psychic power.

Self-deception and the imaginations bred of wishes and emotions are to be guarded against. This is an additional reason for cultivating a tranquil habit of mind and a level-headed habit of judgment. It should be remembered that in solitary Expectancy fraud and trickery are completely absent, and that all manifestations are matters of the most simple personal observation, the accuracy of which can be confirmed—as in an ordinary scientific laboratory—by the test of repetition. For the friends and acquaintances of the sitter the only evidence available is the latter's personal and uncorroborated (statements, which from a scientific point of view are worthless; but for the sitter himself or herself the very same evidence is in the highest degree conclusive, and rightly so. The facts are *known* to have occurred.

3.—The next step after solitary Expectancy has been tried is to arrange with one's friends for Expectancy Circles; that is to say, for groups of persons to meet together at appointed times and in appointed places for the purpose of joint sittings. There are marked advantages in proceeding thus.

First, the probabilities of success are multiplied. It is frequently the case that living individuals, and especially those who have recently lost some relative or friend by death, are "haunted," although they themselves are seldom conscious of the fact. If, then, several persons are present at a sitting the chances of there being some spirits near at hand are much increased.

Secondly, there is a greater likelihood of some person being present who is naturally endowed with mediumistic powers, in which case it becomes easier for a spirit to enter into communication with the sitters.

Thirdly, whatever may be the true explanation of the manner in which manifestations are brought about, it is well known that the more numerous the sitters the more full and complete are the phenomena. The theory of the sitters contributing "electricity" and "personal magnetism" may be very safely rejected as nonsensical; for the very words employed are not used in their ordinary scientific meaning and no other signification has ever been propounded. But each person present does undoubtedly make some contribution to what may be called the common stock of psychical influence available in the room where the sitting takes place.

It should be a matter of common understanding and agreement that the sitters in an Expectancy Circle are all animated by a serious purpose and have not come together for mere amusement or for the "fun" of tricking each other. There is no objection to their being as "sceptical" as they please. A sitter may be of opinion that all occultism is "tomfoolery" and "piffle." Opinions do not alter facts. If psychical phenomena do really occur all the scepticism in the world is of no moment; and no good evidence has ever been brought forward to show that spirits are in any way embarrassed by the presence of doubters and resisters; though it is true enough that passivity on the part of the sitters favours communication. A sceptic may happen to be a good medium without being aware of the fact; in which case his or her mental prejudice will not hinder a spirit from making use of the psychic power thus brought into the Circle. At the same time practical joking and the surreptitious imitation of phenomena are quite out of place. They cannot do any good: they are productive of confusion; and, seeing that discarnate spirits have not changed their minds at death, there does not exist any reason for supposing such beings to have become incapable of taking offence and going away in high dudgeon when sitters attempt to make fools of them—in which case, of course, the sitting is a failure.

With regard to the arrangement of the sitters, this is entirely a matter of convenience. Seats may be provided round a table or scattered about a room. And not the least attention need be paid to the sitters joining hands or being otherwise in contact with each other: the sup-posed necessity of this being a popular delusion based upon some vague and erroneous notion of "electricity." The use of a table is, however, to be recommended. It is desirable for each sitter to have a pencil and paper in readiness; for it cannot be known in advance which par-ticular individuals are capable of automatic writing; and a table facilitates the manifestation as well as providing a convenient standing-place for signalling apparatus, etc.

The sitting may, if desired, take place at high noon-tide and in the very fullest daylight; though, for reasons already stated; it is better to sit in the evening and in semi-obscurity. The singing of hymns, praying and oth-er "religious" features are to be deprecated. They do not affect the actual phenomena; but their tendency is to produce a morbid and emotional frame of mind which in its turn facilitates self-deception and the imaginary perception of happenings that do not really occur. Con-versation also should not be indulged in to any extent that engrosses the attention of the sitters. By far the best plan is for the Circle to sit silently, each individual being on the alert to perceive and announce the slightest indi-cation of anything external.

At the expiration of a few minutes—assuming no manifestation to have happened—some sitter should ask aloud the question, "Is any spirit present?" and if no answer be received the question should be repeated, turn by turn, by all the other sitters. In this way it is often possible to discover those of the Circle who are natural mediums; a fact that is also made evident by the ability to write automatically or by the susceptibility to "impressions," such as touches, whispers, the sensation of a cool breeze, tremblings, twitches and, in rare cases, various forms of clairvoyance, trance and insensibility.

If the first round of questioning produce no result, the silent sitting should be resumed for another period of a few minutes and then the question should again be asked. These alternate silences and questionings should be continued for as long as may be convenient; and then the Circle may adjourn to some future date. It is not, however, very usual for a complete blank to be drawn, where several—say half a dozen or so—persons sit together. Some "sign" or another is pretty sure to be perceived.

When once a manifestation of any kind takes place it should be confirmed by asking for it to be repeated; and then a code of communication can be agreed upon and conversation can proceed. It will facilitate matters and prevent confusion if each communicating spirit be requested to declare its identity, and then for the particular sitter who may recognise the name and personality to conduct the interview.

The so-called "test" questions and other "evidential" conversations are, for the most part, a waste of time and the loss of an opportunity of obtaining useful information. Spirits are, after all, mere ordinary souls in an environment somewhat different from the human body and its mundane surroundings. They are as little likely as is any reasonable man or woman to trouble themselves with personating their fellow-souls at random. What are they to Hecuba, or Hecuba to them? When a spirit claims to be some specified disembodied soul the probabilities are greatly in favour of the claim being true; just as in common life people are found to be as a rule the persons they assert themselves to be. That some of the spirits in circumterrestrial space are, in a sense, vagabonds, without kith, kin or any specific identity connected with humanity, may well be the case, and is now and then a matter of observation; but this is not any reason why they should find any satisfaction in masquerading as Tom, Dick and Harry, There is probably some amusement to be extracted from personating a great figure of history, such as Julius Caesar, Luther, Napoleon, Disraeli or Gladstone, and inducing both mediums and sitters to accept with reverence the pompous utterance of ridiculous banalities; and the history of Spiritualism shows that something of the kind does really happen now and then. But no evidence exists to show that the average sitter who seeks to speak with the average deceased relative or friend is ever duped by any impersonation of the latter. It may not always be possible to prove the genuineness of the communication to the satisfaction of an outside scoffer or critic. This, however, is not a need of the case. The sitter hears and knows for himself or herself at first-hand. What does it matter if outsiders who have not been present at the manifestations and merely hear of them at second-hand choose to evolve from their own inner consciousness the theory that the spirit interviewed was not the real "sainted Maria," but was merely a mischievous "spook" or, more probably, the "fake" of some medium? The old proverb remains good, "The proof of the pudding is in the eating thereof." Any person of ordinary good sense is quite capable of distinguishing between sham and reality even when speaking with the dead is in question.

4.—When an Expectancy Circle has had several successful sittings and has established communications with spirits, those latter should be asked to collect together a group of beings "on the other side" who are willing to co-operate actively with the Circle by regular attendance and the production of manifestations on a continually-developing scale. In past times there has been by far too little of such co-operation. Each professional medium has had his or her alleged "controls," who in an incidental way have occasionally introduced spirits, while the sitters have also—without any design of so doing—brought disembodied souls to the séances. And sittings—especially of the "table" kind—have taken place in private homes where the enquirers have usually been restricted to a few members of a single family, and where the spirits communicated with have been recently-deceased relatives and other inexperienced beings. Under such circumstances it is surprising that so much progress has been made.

It is found, however, that spirits are just as "keen" and interested in psychical phenomena and the extension of communication across the border-line as are the Crookeses, Lodges, Barretts, Crawfords and other investigators in the ranks of the living. It is not difficult for an Expectancy Circle of sitters to develop into a Progressive Circle of co-operating sitters and spirits. A request for co-operation is usually complied with, and it almost always happens that the spirits who are asked to act succeed very quickly in finding others to assist, some of whom have had much experience in manifesting and communicating and can instruct their human colleagues how best to operate. What is chiefly necessary on the part of the sitters in order to ensure results of the highest type is to work in a systematic and co-ordinated way; and the manner in which this may be most effectually done is by each human member of a Progressive Circle entering into relations with some specific spirit-members and undertaking some distinct line of conversation and enquiry by whatever method may be most convenient and practicable—e.g. by automatic or direct writing, by signalling, by clairvoyance, etc. These duologues, or—where more than one sitter and one spirit are concerned—these Committee Meetings may be held at any time and place found fitting, and should be carefully recorded for report to the regular sittings of the Progressive Circle, when the various reports are considered and compared together and are made the starting-point for additional conversations and enquiries,

5.—The great majority of attempts at speaking with the dead are of a character much less ambitious and far-reaching than is that of the Expectancy and Progressive Circles method; and the results are correspondingly imperfect. The system most generally adopted is what in early and mid-Victorian days was known as "table-turning" or "raps," and consisted in a number of persons sitting round a table on which their hands were placed, the right hand of each sitter resting on, or sometimes only touching his neighbour's left hand. After a little while a tapping or rapping noise would be heard on the table, or the table would tilt up a little at intervals, or it would turn round and round, or it would move about the room. Any of these occurrences admitted of utilisation for signalling purposes, and in that way it was found possible to enter into intelligent communication with the spirit or spirits acting on the table—it being generally the case that the communicator was a deceased relative of one of the sitters.

In a Table-sitting—the term now commonly employed—it is desirable for the hands of the sitters to be placed on the table (though the reason for this is not yet clear) , but it is not necessary for any sitter's hands to be in actual contact with those of his neighbours—there not being any electric or other current in circulation. And it is not necessary for the sitters to engage in any form of incantation, whether sung, spoken or thought. They should, however, be serious and attentive, and should be careful not to spoil the sitting by any foolery or conscious attempts to tilt or move the table.

It is best for some one of the sitters to act as spokesman and for some outsider—i.e. a person not sitting at the table—to officiate as the recorder of all that is said and done. The simplest system of communication to adopt is that of the alphabet; the letters being called out by the spokesman in regular order and the table giving a rap or making a movement whenever the right letter is reached. It must not, however, be taken for granted that words will be spelt correctly or that the letters will be grouped in regular sequences of words. Many a message has been put aside as a mere haphazard unmeaning jumble of letters, and has subsequently been found perfectly intelligible and intelligent when the key to the arrangement of the letters has been hit upon. Why such puzzles should be set with seeming deliberation by the spirits is not understood; all we know is that the phenomenon sometimes occurs and its possibility must therefore be taken into account.

6.—The sittings referred to in the foregoing five In-structions are such as may take place without the aid of professional mediums, and for that reason are common-ly regarded as being particularly satisfactory and "evi-dential." This, however, is a view born of prejudice. It assumes that professional mediums are all more or less untrustworthy. Persons who are broad-minded enough to rise superior to prejudice and who choose to weigh seriously the pros and cons of the whole matter are bound to recognise the advantage, in all kinds of en-quiry, of seeking the assistance of individuals possessing natural qualifications who have become expert in their own province. Accordingly, in speaking with the dead a rational person will not deem it needful to keep aloof from professional mediums. Rather will he seek their aid whenever opportunity serves—provided always that no good reason exists for doubting the good faith of any individual medium so met with.

The proceedings at a sitting conducted by a medi-um are of much the same general character as in the case of the Expectancy Circles and Table-sittings al-ready described, except that the sitters are altogether passive instead of taking any active part.

Precautions for ensuring "anonymity" and the like are needless. Mediums as a rule are quite careless re-specting the identity of their sitters, save, perhaps, in the cases of highly-placed persons. Besides, the sitters go to the mediums for their own private requirements and not for the purpose of building up a structure of evidence that shall satisfy some other mind. The best plan, there-fore, is not to trouble about what the medium does or does not know normally, and to depend on one's own common sense in judging of, and dealing with, any communication received.

So, too, with regard to the alleged "controls." It is idle to attempt anything in the nature of cross-examination or "tests." Such attempts, if there be confusion, will only make it worse confounded. The proper course to pursue is to listen attentively to all that is said, and to ask only such questions as may be desirable for the purpose of elucidation or in order to elicit further information.

It is, however, obvious that where a medium writes automatically or speaks under control there must always exist a doubt as to how much is genuine and how much is "sophistication" either intentional or of an unconscious character. The sitter, therefore, who thinks proper to consult a professional medium will do well to ask for a Table-sitting in preference to a Trance-sitting; as when a Table-sitting takes place the medium remains normal, and the communication is conveyed through the instrumentality of the inanimate table instead of making its way amid the disturbing influences of the medium's brain and personality. If the medium cannot, or will not, give a Table-sitting it is not worth while for the sitter to express any dissatisfaction: the situation must be accepted with as good a grace as possible—tranquillity and harmony being the proper atmosphere where mental phenomena are in issue.

In the case of Trance-sittings, where the medium is likely to be strongly controlled and made to speak or act in the guise of some other individuality (it being sometimes the case that a decided modification of facial expression, features and voice becomes noticeable), a frequent practice is to arrange for a subdued light—as, for example, by pulling down the window-blinds and using a lamp with red glass. This is quite unnecessary;

it is a mere conventional usage based upon a tradition to the effect that spirits are more powerful in darkness than in light; but the proceeding need not be objected to. It is as harmless as is the colour or the pattern of the wall-paper.

Some professional mediums adopt the method of Clairvoyance and Clairaudience; that is to say, the communications take the form of an oral description by the medium of what he or she sees and hears in the vicinity of the sitters—the underlying supposition being that the latter bring with them certain haunting spirits or that certain spirits make their way into the room from the outside in order to be near the sitters. This kind of a sitting is, perhaps, the least satisfactory of any from an intellectual point of view. The medium may be labouring under some delusion or may even be deliberately inventing the alleged appearances and utterances. No method has yet been discovered of clearly distinguishing between genuine and unreal clairvoyance (a word which also includes crystal-gazing and the like). Sitters must judge for themselves what to believe and what to reject.

7.—Materialisation-sittings with the assistance of professional mediums form a distinct category of phenomena. They cannot be classed under the head of "communications," and they are just as much physical as psychical. Their chief defect is that they are not "open and above-board," as is the case with the analogous proceedings of ordinary "table-turning" in private circles, where very astounding movements, etc., take place in full light. For some reason or another—good, bad or indifferent—but never on account of any real necessity, materialising mediums in the majority of cases insist upon the sittings taking place in darkness, and upon the use of "cabinets" and screens in the shelter of which the spirits are understood to make their preparations for the show they are about to give. The sitters, of course, cannot interfere: a patient does not instruct the physician with respect to what prescription is needful. Each medium must be allowed to go about his business in his own way; and each sitter is equally free to make his own observations and form his own conclusions.

The stock phenomena in dark séances are the sounding of musical instruments laid upon the table for the purpose and their being moved about through the air, the sitters occasionally feeling themselves touched by the articles in question. Then, too, fitful lights are seen here and there in the room, and voices are heard speaking or singing. Small objects, such as flowers, are tossed about, and larger ones, such as chairs, couches, etc., are moved—often with great violence. It is, moreover, not an uncommon occurrence for detached hands and faces, faintly luminised, to become visible; while, sometimes, what appear to be full-sized simulacra of human beings mix with the sitters.

The medium in charge of such sitting is usually tied to a chair or held by some of the sitters in such as way as to prevent any trickery. This course of action should not, however, be pursued. Sitters do not attend séances for the sake of amusement or for the purpose of witnessing a clever conjuring exhibition. There ought not to be any question of a contest of wits between the sitters and the medium. The real object to be striven for is the completeness of the manifestations; and this can best be attained by giving the medium and the spirits the freest of free play.

Let it be granted, for argument's sake, that trickery is possible. Let it be admitted, as a matter of fact, that many mediums have been detected and exposed in various instances of imposture. This shows merely that some alleged materialisations are not genuine; it does not prove that no materialisation ever takes place. Here, also, the sitter must judge for himself. Where it is possible to adopt both a normal and a supernormal explanation of any observed manifestation the rules of scientific enquiry impose upon us the obligation of postulating a "natural" cause in preference to assuming that some "supernatural" power is in operation; we are bound, for example, in cases admitting of trickery, to hold that the medium is a cheat rather than to infer the intervention of any spirit. But when a normal explanation is not possible, or so highly improbable as to be outside the confines of good sense, we act foolishly if we insist upon declining to recognise a patent fact merely because it does not fit in with our pre-conceived opinions. The same remark applies, mutatis mutandis, to many of the "normal explanations" in themselves. It is, for example, said sometimes that the voices heard in the course of dark sittings are produced ventriloquially by the medium. This leaves out of view the consideration that ventriloquy is in itself an illusion depending upon the sense of sight as well as upon that of hearing. No ventriloquist, however clever, can produce the impression of there being a sound emanating from some specific locality when the hearer is in the dark; a fact that is evident to any person who tries the experiment of shutting his eyes when at a ventriloquial entertainment. And if we reflect that in a materialisation seance several distinct voices are often heard simultaneously, the explanation of the medium being a ventriloquist is seen to be ludicrously inadequate. The "normal" theory does not fare any better in suggesting that the medium manages to vacate his chair in the darkness and to pick up the trumpet or the tambourine, etc., from which he forthwith proceeds to extract some sounds. This might be feasible in the case of a single instrument in a single locality; but it often happens that several instruments of various kinds are being played simultaneously and are heard in different parts of the room at the same time. And when it is remembered that the sitting where such facts occur may, and does frequently, take place in a sit-ter's own house, where the medium has not been able to make any preparations and where no confederate is available, the futility of the "natural" way of accounting for the manifestations becomes still further evident. So, after all, we come round once more to the recommen-dation that the sitter should not interfere, should merely observe, should keep an open mind and should be guid-ed by facts quite irrespectively of whether the facts be normal or super-normal.

CHAPTER VIII

"SPIRITUALISM" AND "RATIONALISM"

This book ought not to be concluded without something being said as to its design and character, and as to the mental attitude it presumes on the part of its readers.

It is intended, first, as a practical guide for the assistance of those persons who may be desirous of speaking with the dead; and, secondly, as an elementary text-book of occult phenomena. It presupposes for its readers a willingness to be guided by facts and a disregard of opinions based upon imagination instead of upon fact.

Leaving out of view all questions of religion, religious authority and Church controversy, it may be stated generally that most people are given to understand that occult matters must be looked upon in the light of either "spiritualism" or "rationalism." When, therefore, they find in the public press various statements by eminent spiritualists that demolish the case of the rationalists, and when they at the same time discover statements by eminent rationalists that are equally destructive of the positions occupied by the spiritualists, it becomes very difficult for persons who are not close students of the matters in dispute to arrive at a settled judgment. Accordingly, the following observations may prove of some service.

The true nature of articles in the newspapers, magazines and reviews should be borne in mind. These articles are written professionally, that is, for pay, and they have to provide commercial value for the remuneration received by their writers. They have to be readable and popular, which means that they must be smart and sensational and penned with much literary ability. The authors have also their own futures to think of; they must please their respective editors and they must show off to the best advantage such stores of knowledge, such dialectical powers, and such capabilities in the arts of sarcasm and abuse as they may possess. They are like the barristers in the courts of law. They are not concerned for either justice or truth. Their business is to snatch a verdict if they can; and to do this they find their best plan is to fasten upon the weak points of their adversaries and ignore the strong ones; while, as regards their own cases, they make the most of every favourable feature and keep all doubtful points in the background. So the reader should be on his or her guard, and should not accept meekly, as a matter of course, anything that appears in print. A good example of what is here referred to may be found in the *Strand Magazine* of July, 1917, under the title of "Is Sir Oliver Lodge Right? 'Yes,' by Sir A. Conan Doyle. 'No,' by Edward Clodd."

Persons who wish to pursue the study of dialectics and partisan literature in connection with psychical phenomena may be recommended to read *Light* and *The*

International Psychic Gazette, which are the two leading organs of the Spiritualists in England, and the *Literary Guide* (the sub-title being *The Rationalist Review*), which is published by the Rationalist Press Association, and is the recognised mouthpiece of the most distinguished exponents of Rationalism in the United Kingdom. All three of the publications referred to are characterised by much learning and very great ability. The facts they record are selected carefully from partisan points of view and the comments and arguments that appear in their pages are admirably one-sided and correspondingly conclusive. But the reader is thus enabled to see both sides of the shield, and has himself only to blame if he become the champion of either gold or silver.

Current literature, however, is not the only danger in the path of persons who desire to walk in the company of Reason. Current teaching is perhaps even more formidable, and especially so where Science is concerned. The popular idea of scientific men is that they are votaries of Truth and are deaf to the voice of every other deity. Hence the authority wielded by the leaders of Science, and the willing obedience rendered to their behests. It is rarely remembered that scientific men are simple human beings, subject to the same weaknesses and possessed of the same foibles as the rest of the race. History has shown that if power be placed in the hands of any professional set of men it will inevitably be abused; and Science does not provide an exception to the rule. There is every whit as much bigotry, blind dogma and savage intolerance in scientific circles as ever there was in any ecclesiastical or puritanical organisations. Sir William Crookes, O.M., P.R.S., found this out very many years ago, and Sir Oliver Lodge, F.R.S., is now rediscovering it; the latter case of persecution by the Rationalistic Inquisition being rendered particularly piquant because of the great indebtedness of current materialism to the famous champion of the Ether—a doctrine that forms the only line of defence as yet available against the attacks of the Becquerel rays, the Ballistic Theory of Explosives and other subverters of modern dogma.

In the midst of all such strife this little book is neutral, and it counsels its readers to be neutral also. Rationalism is a good thing in a way and within proper limits; and so is Spiritualism. But neither the one nor the other is the whole truth; and, when rightly understood, the two schools of thought are not at variance. When Science speaks of the universe being fashioned and ruled by Nature, Evolution and the like, it is only another way of naming the very same existing something that the Christian calls God. The glorious Service of Humanity when followed into the recesses of its meaning is found to be a mere plain listening to one's conscience; and the survival of good deeds is, in the last analysis, indistinguishable from the survival of the souls by whom they are accomplished.

Sursum corda. Let us speak to the dead and let us add their knowledge and counsel to the common store.

THE END

*9 7 8 1 7 3 5 3 2 0 1 0 6 *